A
DAISY FOR
DOROTHY

This book is for Dorothy, for George and Nan,
for all who go to war and those who wave goodbye.

A
DAISY FOR
DOROTHY

THE LOVE STORY OF A
FAMILY IN WARTIME
PAT READ
INTRODUCTION BY
LESLIE THOMAS

BLOOMSBURY

First published 1989

Copyright © Pat Read 1989

Bloomsbury Publishing Ltd, 2 Soho Square, London W1V 5DE

A CIP catalogue record for this book is available from
the British Library.

ISBN 0 7475 0454 7

10 9 8 7 6 5 4 3 2

Designed by Malcolm Smythe
Photoset by Rowland Phototypesetting Ltd
Bury St Edmunds, Suffolk
Printed in Great Britain by
Butler and Tanner Ltd, Frome and London

Contents

INTRODUCTION
by Leslie Thomas

The chronicles of war are not always writ large. For all the bound volumes of history, the excuses of the politicians and the explanations of field marshals, there are boundless pieces of paper, notes and diaries and letters, which tell the story in small and occasionally deathly prose. Some of the most poignant records of D-Day in 1944, muddied and bloodied still, written on message pads while under fire on the Normandy beaches, I have found folded away in the US Army Archives in Washington DC.

A Daisy For Dorothy, a touching collection of letters written throughout the war between an ordinary soldier-husband and his wife, comes into the same category. Even their names, George and Nan Scragg, might have been thought appropriate had this – as it well might – been written as a novel. George was born in the first month of the First World War, and was killed in action in the final few days of the Second World War. His commanding officer believes that his letter of condolence to Nan was probably the last he had to write. At the end, the sense of ordinary tragedy is almost unbearable, even though it happened now many years ago.

They came from neighbouring Midland villages, George and Nan, where the men worked in pits or pottery. Nan fell in love with him because of his tall stature and manly looks, the very attributes which sent him eventually to his death. After going through most of the war in a series of mundane domestic postings, he was picked out for infantry training before the invasion of Normandy. George was almost thirty – an 'old man' in infantry terms – but because of his physique and conscientious fitness, he was put into the sharp end of the fighting. His letters made it plain that he did not want to go, but as Pat Read says in her narrative, he was fit and he was obedient; he was, in other words, cannon fodder.

The Scraggs come across, through their letters written two or three times a week, as exceptional though simple people. Both were highly moral and proper – irritatingly so at times – and ready to exchange scornful judgements, he on other soldiers, she on her fellow villagers. She worries that he may have dealings with other women. The soldiers billeted have behaved scandalously and, apparently, with the full co-operation of local girls. He watches his comrades go eagerly off the rails and wonders why they do it. A small beer, a game of solo and a visit to the pictures is enough for him. He only begins to smoke – and shamefacedly confesses it – when he is about to go into action and the cigarettes are distributed as a sop.

Their concerns are the little house they will share some day after the war. (They voice a not-often acknowledged sadness of the time; there was no definite time-limit on the interruption of their lives but only a vague 'when all this is over' yearning.) Their daughter, the Dorothy of the title, is born after much computation of twenty-four-hour leaves so that they might coincide with the maximum opportunity for Nan to become pregnant.

They discuss the big war and their own small wars. George never seems to have been hampered by the imposition of censorship, although when he was in action he preferred not to discuss it. In the village, life and death go on much as usual: the weather changes, Christmas (sometimes beerless) comes and goes, children are born, marriages start and finish, a boy and then a girl are drowned in the canal.

These are the ordinary thoughts of an ordinary, but ultimately, tragic couple. As he walked away from her on his final leave Nan said, 'That's it. I shan't see him again.' George's final line was prosaic as ever. It said: 'Give my love to all at home.'

The Scragg family in the mid 1930s. Back row from left: George, Job Scragg, Mary Meacham, Les Meacham; front row: Mary Osborne, Emma Scragg, Dennis Meacham [baby], Nan.

THE PEOPLE IN THE STORY

The Scragg Family

George Scragg, killed in action in Germany, 26 April 1945

Florence Ann Scragg, née Osborne, George's wife, known as Nan

Dorothy, their daughter, born February 1943, now Mrs White

Job Scragg, a coalminer, and his wife Emma, George's parents

Mary Meacham, née Scragg, George's sister; Les Meacham, her husband; Dennis, their son

The Osborne Family

Joe Osborne, landlord of the Swan Inn at Armitage, Nan's father

Florrie Osborne, Joe's wife

Mary Yardley, née Osborne, Nan's twin sister

Ted Yardley, Mary's husband and George's friend; David, their son, born September 1941

John Osborne, known as 'Jack', Nan's brother; his wife Ada

Dolly Timmis, née Osborne, Nan's sister; her husband Frank

Nora Smith, née Osborne, Nan's sister; her husband Jack

The Middleton Family

Stan Middleton, George's best friend in the Scots Guards
Minnie Middleton, Stan's mother

FOREWORD

As clearly as a piece of film unreeling, the memory un-winds; I am very small, maybe three years old. I am standing in the bedroom window of the little house where I was born, looking out towards the railway. A train is pulling down the line away from me and a man in uniform is leaning out of the window, waving.

Someone, probably my mother, is saying, 'Wave to Daddy.' Something ceremonial is happening; I feel it is important, but I am not sad. The man called Daddy is a stranger. The rough wool of his uniform is scratchy; it makes him smell alien. The train takes him, still waving, round the curve of the track and out of sight.

Wave to Daddy. Wave bye-bye.

My friend Dorothy's father did not return. She was only two years old when he was killed, and she cannot remember him. But the shadow of his absence has dom-inated her life. The tin trunk in which Dorothy's mother hoarded all her mementoes during nearly forty years of widowhood was such a powerful symbol of that loss that, after her mother's death, Dorothy felt unable to face tackling its contents and she asked me to do it for her.

The trunk was a mess, a jumbled mass of 2,000 letters, documents, photographs, greetings cards and other sou-venirs. The first priority was to read all the letters and put them into chronological order. Many were written in pencil and were fading; most were undated although, luckily, many were still in their original envelopes, so the postmarks helped. Sometimes reference to an event in the news provided the clue, sometimes a family occasion fitted it into the jigsaw.

In editing the letters, I have tried to interfere with their contents as little as possible, occasionally tidying punctuation and avoiding repetition, besides selecting those which told the story as clearly as I could. This was the story of Nan and George and I wanted to tell it with their voices and on their terms.

During the two years it took to complete the work, researching the events of the war, tracing and interviewing the witnesses, I developed a fierce and protective love for Nan and George. Their letters are simple and honest and that candour reveals their faults as well as their love, but, above all, they are thoroughly ordinary and innocent. They were sentimental people, so it is a sentimental book, for which I make no apology. Ordinary people are sentimental; that is why they have paid, and continue to pay, the price of war.

Those in authority do not like us to count that cost – how, otherwise, would they persuade us to fight again? Wounded veterans are excluded from victory parades. Nan's obsessive mourning provoked disapproval; her behaviour was contrary to good order and discipline, bad for morale, constantly tearing at her wounds and displaying them like stigmata. She was not a brave little soldier.

Through this book, Dorothy was able, for the first time, to understand something of the lives of the father she had never known and the mother she had tried in vain to comfort. It is a small-scale story, tiny voices of the true unknown warriors. Multiply it a million times, in many tongues, and it echoes still with awesome power around the world.

George and Nan courting, probably in 1935.

Chapter One

'It's a Lovely Day Tomorrow'

The soldier's name was George Scragg. He had neither intended to join the army nor had taken active steps to avoid it; like many others, he was fighting because those in authority had told him it was necessary. This was a period of the twentieth century when soldiering became a job for ordinary citizens, rather than one for a relatively small group of men who chose it as a profession.

George's war was the Second World War, fought between 1939 and 1945 when, for the second time in 30 years, the scale of the conflict and the efficiency of the weapons available were beyond the capacity of the professional military. Within a few years, advancing technology would again turn the tables, rendering vast numbers of soldiers obsolete and causing the citizens' armies to be disbanded.

The Second World War was a struggle of ideologies, transforming global politics and the lives of a generation. But as a combat soldier George's role was simple. He went where he was sent, obeyed orders and wished the war would end so he could go home. Home was where his wife and baby daughter were, in the small Staffordshire village of Armitage in the Midlands. George had been born two miles away in the next-door village of Brereton, the younger of two children of Job Scragg, a coalminer, and his wife Emma, in September 1914, just as an earlier great conflict was beginning.

As the precious only son, born in his mother's later years, George claimed a special place in her heart, and she expressed her feelings in small, practical pamperings. When, at the age of fourteen, George started work, she would warm his trousers in front of the fire before he got up on a winter morning – an indulgence which astonished his wife's family when they learned of it.

George did not follow his father down the pit outside Brereton village, but began a five-year apprenticeship as a potter, learning how to cast lavatory bowls and washbasins for the district's second major employer after the mines, the bathroom fittings manufacturer Edward Johns and Company Limited, which later became Armitage Shanks. It was known locally as the 'potbank' or the 'bank', and unwittingly gave its name to the 'John'.

By the time he was in his teens, George was an attractive young man, nearly six feet tall, with thick, dark, curly hair of which he seemed to be very proud, since he left it free of the heavy, greasy dressing with which many young men of his generation flattened and tamed theirs. Although liked by his workmates, George was never 'one of the lads'; his natural reserve, strong religious convictions

George's birth certificate.

and a certain puritan streak – which he shared with his wife – made him disapprove of excess.

'George was a very pleasant bloke to be with,' said brother-in-law Ted Yardley, who started work at the 'pot-bank' at the same time. 'He was very shy and, though he was good-looking, I don't think he'd had a girlfriend before he started courting Nan, and it took a lot of persuading before he would go and meet the family. He enjoyed a game of darts and cards, but he really liked to do quiet things like fishing and gardening. He never drank more than a couple of bottles of stout.'

It was not timidity which gave George his sense of reserve; Ted remembered that his friend was not one to suffer fools gladly. 'George could be quite short-tempered. Not that he ever got into real trouble, but he always spoke his mind if there was something he didn't agree with, and that made it hard for him when he went into the Army. He didn't like the discipline in the Army, and, of course, you can't show your temper there. I didn't mind it so much, because I was more easy-going. But George, if something upset him, would go up like a bottle of pop. With him being so much younger than his sister, I think his mother spoiled him a little. He was always treated like a baby of the family, and it was a big change being away from home. In those days, we weren't used to travelling or even working away from home. We all had to accept it, but George never cared for it, although he was always well-disciplined at home.'

George in 1931, aged seventeen, at work at Edward Johns, which later became Armitage Shanks.

George's work registration card.

Perhaps George's reticence was connected with a fastidiousness about his appearance. 'He was very smart,' said Ted, 'always neatly dressed, his shoes polished, wearing the stiff collars his mother starched for him; always checking his tie was straight and his hair was properly combed.'

15

The 'potbank'.

Making toilets at Edward Johns between the wars.

Florence Annie Osborne, known to her family as 'Nan', was sixteen when she first noticed George. The curls may have been the attraction, or it may have been his height that caught her eye, since he must have stood head and shoulders above most of the small, wiry youngsters in the industrial villages of that time. He towered over Nan, who was slender and barely five feet tall – a disparity which gives an endearing, lopsided look to the snapshots taken of them during their courtship as George bends and tucks his shoulder down to meet her.

Nan was one of five children of Joe and Florrie Osborne, who ran the Swan Inn in the centre of Armitage, just across the road from the entrance to the 'potbank'.

The Swan Inn during the First World War; Joe Osborne is standing outside with Dolly and Nora.

'We were the babies of the family – my Dad always said we were the scrapings of the barrel,' her twin Mary recalled. 'Although Nan was older than me, she was always the weak one. She just never seemed to be quite well. She had scarlet fever when she was little and an overactive thyroid, and she was never very strong. But I think my mother spoiled her a bit, and we sometimes felt that she used not being well to get out of doing her share of the work. She and I helped in the pub after we left school, cleaning, and later behind the bar. It was hard and neither of us liked it much.'

Nan was a bright, pretty girl, popular in the village. She once won a white angora rabbit after being chosen as the best-liked girl in her school.

'She loved dancing and the boys liked her. She was a bit of a flirt, in a nice way, and always liked to know what was going on in the village,' said Mary.

Nan and Mary with their nurse.

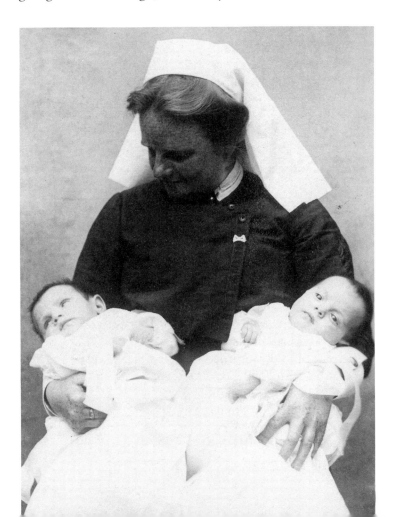

The Osborne family in 1918 or early 1919; left to right: John, Nan, Florrie, Nora, Joe, Mary and Dolly.

Although deeply religious, Nan also took notice of the superstitions common among country people. She knew all the disasters that would certainly follow broken mirrors, spilled salt, umbrellas opened in the house and May blossom brought indoors. It is hardly surprising that, throughout her life, Nan had a strong feeling that potent forces were at work, shaping events that were 'meant to be'. The first time she noticed George Scragg there was not only a powerful, physical attraction, but also an equally strong sense of 'fate', as approved by her favourite romantic magazine stories and Hollywood films, even if it needed a helping hand.

'Nan was in the street with another girl when she saw George,' Mary recalled. 'She said to her friend, "I want him. That's the one I'm going to marry." And she got him.'

Engineering a meeting was simple, even for a strictly brought up girl, living at home. There was the carefully planned 'accident' of just happening to be walking by with a friend as the factory turned out, and the message relayed through friends, 'Tell George she likes him and she'll be at the dance on Saturday night.'

George did not like dancing. 'It was strange that they met at a dance,' said Mary. 'Nan loved it, but George was never keen. I don't think he went again often after they met,

Nan, aged fifteen, outside Armitage Church around the time she first saw George.

because he used to sit out and he was very jealous when Nan danced with other boys, and I think that put a stop to it as far as Nan was concerned.'

Ted Yardley, who began to court Mary at about the same time, remembered, 'There was a song that was popular at the time, "Two little Girls in Blue", and Nan was always very fond of wearing blue. Some of the lads at work teased George by singing it after Nan had danced with other boys and he just blew his top.'

The courtship and engagement continued for five years, with long walks, bus trips to the next town to see a film, family Sunday teas and the occasional and carefully chaperoned seaside holidays with family and friends.

They were a handsome couple, said Mary. 'Nan always liked to be fashionable. I remember there was a craze for little tilted hats like the ones Princess Marina, the Duchess of Kent, wore, and Nan had to have one. She even did her hair up at the back like Princess Marina. George always looked smart. They looked good together.

'George just idolised her. He wouldn't hear any of us say a word against her, and Nan really loved him. They were both rather sentimental people. George's favourite song was "Danny Boy", and afterwards, Nan could never bear to hear it. She always ran from the room when she heard it played. When he went away, she kept a photograph of him by her bedside and she kissed him goodnight every night of her life until his face was worn away.'

Nan and George, and Mary and Ted, were married in a double ceremony at the village church in February 1939, when the twins were twenty-one. Although the Osborne family owned several houses in the village, only one was then vacant and, as Ted Yardley was living in lodgings, the family decided that the new Mr and Mrs Yardley should have it. Nan and George moved into the pub with Nan's parents to wait for a second cottage to become available.

'We never thought anything like the war would happen,' Mary said. 'We imagined that we would live all our lives in the village. George and Nan were happy together. She was devoted to him and she needed him, needed someone to look after her. He was the one who made all the decisions and did all the organising. She was never any good on her own.'

George and Nan, late 1930s.

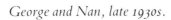

Ted Yardley and George, 1936–37.

21

The wedding report in the Lichfield Mercury.

HELLO, TWINS!
INTERESTING
DOUBLE WEDDING
AT ARMITAGE

A very pretty wedding, which attracted more than usual local interest, took place at the Parish Church, Armitage, on Wednesday week, when the twin daughters of Mr. and Mrs. J. H. Osborne, the popular host and hostess of the Swan Inn were married. The service was conducted by the Rev. F. Keith Lawrence (Rector), and Miss Florence Anne Osborne was married to Mr. George Scragg, whose parents reside at Brereton, and Miss Winifred Mary Osborne to Mr. Edward John Yardley, whose parents, formerly well-known residents, now live at Wolverhampton.

The brides, who were given away by their father, were charmingly attired in white silk velvet, their embroidered net veils being suspended from head-dresses of orange blossom, and they carried bouquets of arum lilies. There were four bridesmaids and one little page in attendance. The two elder bridesmaids, Miss Edith Whitwell (Manchester) and Miss Olive Maltby (Derby) both friends of the brides, wore dresses of old gold silk velvet with halo hats trimmed with violets, and carried posies of violets, and the two smaller ones, Miss Heather Smith (niece of the brides) and Miss Hazel Churmaize (niece of the bridegroom), also looked very sweet in dresses of duck egg blue velvet with hats to match, and carried posies of snowdrops. The page, Master Dennis Meacham, nephew of the bridegroom, wore a beige satin blouse with velvet trousers.

The duties of best man to Mr. Yardley were carried out by Mr. Bernard King, Armitage, and to Mr. Scragg by Mr. H. Haycock, Brereton.

The service was fully choral, Mr. A. C. Renshaw officiating at the organ. The hymns "O Perfect Love" and "Thine for Ever" were sung. Following the ceremony a reception was held at the Swan Inn, Armitage, which was attended by upwards of fifty guests.

MERRY NALGO

Mary and Nan's double wedding, 8 February 1939.

In September 1939, Britain declared war on Hitler's Germany, and a year later George and Ted were conscripted into the army.

'When we knew we were going to be called up,' said Ted, 'the manager called nine of us young men together and gave us the sack. He said there wasn't much work, as nobody was building houses because of the war and we were going to be called up anyway, so he would have to let us go. He advised us to try to get into munitions work so that we needn't go in the army, but neither George nor I wanted that. In fact, George's Dad wanted him to go down the pit so that he would be exempt. He even went so far as to buy George a pair of boots to wear, but George refused.

'George and I never talked about politics, and I don't know how he would have voted, but we had read in the newspapers about Hitler taking over the continent and we didn't want it to happen here. We thought it was our duty to go in the army and do our share.'

After a short time working on a new airfield under development a few miles away, their call-up came and they set off together, leaving home for the first time, to join the Royal Artillery as part of the defences for the airfields of East Anglia.

Mary said, 'Nan and George never really had a proper married life. They never had their own home because the cottage they were to have had did not become vacant, and they had been living with my parents at the pub until George went away. Ted and I had our own home, where we could be in private, before he went in the army and when he came on leave. I have always felt that Nan was the pretty twin, but I was the lucky one.'

The letters that Nan and George wrote to each other twice a week for the next four years became in effect the whole of their relationship; the account these letters give of their lives is extremely poignant. The mixture of dreams and gossip, memories and stark reality that the couple recorded became virtually their only private life, the more so since their home was the village inn – literally a public house – where they were constantly under the eyes of relatives and customers, even during the leaves snatched from George's war duties. It is little wonder the letters were so precious to Nan that she hoarded them for nearly forty years with all the fanaticism of a squirrel which knows a long winter is coming.

With such gentle and seductive links, Nan bound herself to her past and to her dreams, eventually encircling her own present and her family's future. These links were as beguiling as the chains made from the daisies George was to pick with his much-loved daughter Dorothy; but they were chains nonetheless.

George going off to war.

Chapter Two

'You're in the Army Now'

George, 1940

Whatton-in-the-Vale
Nottingham
17 September

Dear Nan

Just a note to let you know we have arrived safely. I should say there was about 100 – 150 come in today from all about the country, some from the Potteries. We had to wait 2½ hours at Nottingham, arriving there at 12 o'clock. We have been before the MO, had tea and been issued with most of our kit. Well, sweetheart, there isn't much to report. We are all right, so don't worry, duck. I can't give you an address as I don't know my number, so I shall write again when I have it.

It's nearly blackout, so I'll go and find the post box before it's too dark, duck.

Goodnight, darling, sleep sound, don't upset yourself, goodnight.

From your loving husband George xxxxxx

Just heard there is only one post per day, ¼ past 5, so it's too late tonight, dear. Sweet dreams. Give my love to all, duck.

Whatton-in-the-Vale
18 September

I'm writing again dear to say you have no need to worry,
as we are having good meals and beds to kip down on,
wardrobes to put our belongings in. The chaps are lying
about like dead sheep tonight. We have been vaccinated
and nocculated this morning after visiting the dental
bloke.

We are being issued with plenty of kit, 3 pair of socks,
2 vests, 3 shirts, 2 pairs of pants, scarf, pullover, 1 pair of
pumps, 2 of boots, clothes brush, shaving brush, gym
vests and pants and it's all good stuff.

We have had roll call and been split into squads of 15.
Ted and myself worked out to be in the same lot, so it's
OK.

K Squad
Whatton-in-the-Vale
20 September

We are still confined to barracks, but we might be allowed
out tomorrow night. There was a concert party come last
night to entertain us from Nottingham and it was quite a
decent show and gave us a chance to forget the gammy
arm for an hour or two. But I think they are improving,
not so much groaning or bad language today.

Well, duck, the food is champion, no rationing here,
plenty of meat and butter. In fact there is a lot of it goes
begging. It's pay-day tomorrow, sweetheart, but at the
present rate of spending I shall be able to send you some
instead of you sending me.

From your everloving
George x x x x x x

PS I'm looking forward to a letter from you, dear.
Tell the solo players Ted and me would not mind making
up some night when they are short.

Whatton-in-the-Vale
22 September

Well, sweetheart, I've been sitting here about ten minutes
wondering what to put in this letter. We had a church
parade this morning. They marched us to Bingham and on
the return, the captain halted all groups and supposed we
were being attacked by enemy aircraft. You ought to see
the rush for the ditch. Some had a good trampling on.

    We had a big pay bag on Friday, 5/–, still I haven't
changed the 4s PO or the £1 note, so I'm OK for money.

    Well, dear, I'm still waiting for that first letter. It
seems awful without a line from you, but patience is a
virtue, duck, although I might receive it before you get
this.

[In her first letter to George, Nan had exciting news; a house
belonging to a relative had unexpectedly become vacant and
it was offered to George and Nan. She asks George whether
they should take it, or wait until he comes home. George's
reluctance for them to accept was ultimately to have far-
reaching consequences. Firstly, it meant they never had the
home of their very own which they so longed for; the
snatched days George and Nan spent together during
the War were inevitably shared with family and with the
patrons of the Swan Inn, and the couple never experienced a
'normal' married life. Also, Nan was sheltered from many
of the day-to-day harsh realities of life through living with
her parents and later her twin Mary, and therefore never
really developed the sense of independence she needed to
buffer her from future events.]

Whatton-in-the-Vale
23 September

I was very pleased when the bombardier called my name
out this morning, worth more than £5 to me, darling, for I
can sit and read it time and again. I've read it every chance
I've had this afternoon. Well, sweet, it has lifted a load off
my mind to know you are feeling better. Keep it up, duck.
As for me, I've never felt fitter.

Now, about the house, pidge, I think it better to let it slide for these two or three reasons. First of all, I think it would cause you a lot of worry without me being with you. Secondly, I don't want to keep a white elephant as times are, darling, and as you say you are comfortable where you are, don't you think it's best to let it slide too? It was very nice of Aunt and Uncle to give us the first chance. Tell them I thank them and don't be afraid to explain, dear.

Duck, all I've written about the conditions here is quite true, you could not wish for better. We are all good pals in our barrack room in which there are 30 men, and are we downhearted? I'll say we are not!

It's getting near to lights out, dear, and I've got some jobs to do before morning, two pair of socks to wash, a pair of boots to clean and a bit of polishing. We've got to send our big washing to a laundry in Nottingham and we could send our socks, but the SM advises to wash them ourselves. I've just parcelled mine up for the morning's collection. Oh, it just reminded me, bring some marking ink and a pen, darling. They will do when you come. Goodnight, darling, and God bless you. Sweet dreams and hope for the best.

The Searchlights unit in 1941–42; George is second from the right in the front row.

Whatton-in-the-Vale
27 September

Well, darling, we have just been noc. again and that means 48 hours confined to barracks and 6 o'clock Sunday evening before anyone can go out, but that won't make a lot of difference to me as I've only been out once. Sweetheart, I think we shall be having a weekend off next week, so if you don't come this Sunday, I shouldn't bother next if I were you, duck.

They are squeezing every minute that comes with drill, hardly time to get from our meals before it's 'On parade, you chaps!' But still it's worth it, dear, if it gets us a short leave. I *shall* be glad to see you, darling. It seems a lifetime since we were together, but we shan't always be parted, pidge.

I hope you are not disappointed, darling about the house, but when this ruddy job is over and we're back to

civvy street again, we'll have that dream house of ours,
sweet, and start to enjoy life as it should be.

Goodnight and God Bless you, dear, sweet dreams.
From your everloving sweetheart
George x x x x x x x

PS I haven't had a drink, or played cards, darling. I
think instead of changing for the worse, it's for the better
and I can do without both with no trouble.

Whatton-in-the-Vale
30 September

Well, darling, I'll start off with a line or two of good news.
All being well, sweetheart, I shall be with you this
weekend, as we are probably having a 51 hr leave from 7
o'clock Fri to 10 o'clock Sun night. So if you hear banging
on the door, you will know who it is, duck. It will be
great, dear, to have you near, if it is only for so short a
time. I'm living for Friday.

Whatton-in-the-Vale
8 October

I am writing this note in a hurry. It's our 20 min. break.
Well, darling, we got back all right, but we had to get a lift
to Derby and from there we got various buses until we
were 2½ miles from camp. We started to walk it, but were
not sure of the right direction as we got off one bus at
X-roads, so we decided to go back to enquire. We hadn't
got back to them before we saw a bus coming our way, so
I waved the torch and stopped it, and damn me if it wasn't
the Pottery bus we should have come back on. After
putting us off at Uttoxeter they had a whip round for the
driver so that he would give them an extra hour in the
Potteries, so they didn't start from there till 8 o'clock
instead of 7. We had waited until ¼ to 9 for them and
given it up then. It was nearly 12 before we got to camp,
but there are some of the chaps still rolling in now, so we
were lucky.

Well, sweetheart, time's nearly up, so ta-ra, duck. I

will write a letter tomorrow. Excuse this scribble, but I can't help it under the circumstances. So long, remember me to them all and thank them.

Whatton-in-the-Vale
8 October

Well, duck, it's still Monday as I write this letter, but I've more time to tell you about last night's escapade, which ended up alright, nothing being said to us. Some are still away. They will get it hot, I'll tell you, and it's that sort of behaviour that will do us harm for another leave, but our Captain is leaving us on Fri and the one that's pretty lenient with leaves is taking over, so let's hope for the best.

Sweetheart, I'm glad you didn't wait with us last night, for I know how worried you would have been about it. We thought it was a night out ourselves. However, a motor car came up the same way as we came, so we waved and it pulled up. I asked how far they were going and it was Derby, and how surprised I was when the fellow switched the inside light on, for there was him and his wife, with one little boy in the front seat, one asleep on the back, with a little sister asleep in a cradle by his side. I apologised for stopping them and said we would wait for another, but they insisted we should get in. So the woman took the boy out of the back seat and put him on her knees and I had the baby and cradle on mine. They said we were the third couple to have a lift, two Czech airmen before us, so I think it was very good of them under the circumstances, don't you, pidge?

Darling, yesterday was one of the brightest spots of my life, but oh, the parting! I can't explain, it's not a job for a pen or pencil. To hold and kiss you in my arms was just heaven after those three weeks. You've no idea what it meant to me, love. I'm living for the next time and hoping it won't be long.

From your everloving sweetheart
George x x x x x

Darling I *do* love you.

Whatton-in-the-Vale
12 October

We went on a 3 hour field craft route march yesterday,
over ploughed fields, streams and lots of other obstacles,
getting to our objectives without being observed in a
mock raiding party. I slept like a top last night, tired out,
but we enjoyed it better than the square. Our Captain
went to fresh quarters today. The R S M [Regimental
Sergeant Major] and a 2nd Lieutenant have come to take
over, with all new ideas about the drills.
     From your everloving sweetheart
     George x x x x x x x

     Keep smiling, pidge. It won't last forever. I was
dreaming about you Monday night, dear, such a lovely
dream. We had agreed to you know what, darling, and
it was great. I shall be glad when we can in reality,
sweetheart.

O Squad
Whatton-in-the-Vale
[Undated]

Thank you very much for the parcel, love. It *was* a
surprise. I only expected a letter. The mug is OK, I've just
tried it at teatime and the tea tastes a lot better out of it.
Tell Mary we shall enjoy her tarts and cake. It brings home
a bit nearer, you know, love. And thank Doll for the
gloves, they will be very welcome in the near future as it
goes real cold now at nights. The mirror was intact, but
the cheese biscuits were all smashed up, so I shouldn't send
anymore of those, duck. I'm well off for stamps now,
pidge. I'd only used about two out of the book your
mother gave me, so I shan't want any for a time, but thank
you for your book, dear.
     Take care of yourself this cold weather. Wear
something warm and keep a good pair of shoes on. I don't
forget your little tricks, you know, love, but you *will* take
care, won't you?
     Well, darling I don't really know when we move, but
it's rumoured that the coming week is our last here. I shall

33

let you know when we get it official, love, and if there is a leave next weekend, which I *do* hope there is.

We haven't been out this week yet, but Ted and myself might go tonight for a drink. It was awful last night. They were coming in absolutely helpless and there was a few black eyes on show this morning. Silly devils, I call them. Two lots got confined to barracks through it. Ours will be the next from what I can see about it, but the innocent have to suffer as well, which I don't think is right. Still it's the Army all over.

Whatton-in-the-Vale
16 October

I've got a sore throat, going to the MO's three times today to gargle it, but it feels a lot better tonight, pidge. Ted's been and had his teeth scraped today. My turn can't be far away now and I don't fancy the visit I can tell you.

Well, darling, I hope you arrived back safe on Sunday night. It was a lovely night, wasn't it, dear? A proper lovers' night, moon shining. My thoughts went back to the same sort when we were courting, love. The nights seem awful here, sweet. The moon's shining, but we've no inclination to go out. I shall be glad when we are able to go for a nice walk together again, darling.

Intake 367 Battery
St Hugh's School
Woodhall Spa
Lincolnshire
[Undated: 22 October?]

Darling, as you can see by the address, we have made our move. We got here ½ past 8 last night. It was a rotten journey, leaving camp just after 3 to catch the 3-41 from Aslockton.

Well, sweetheart, I can't give you much about the place yet, only that it's an evacuated private school and taken over roughly by about 240 men. It don't seem too bad. The biggest setback is that I can't come to see you so often, darling. But never mind, duck, you are with me *all* the while. Ted and I are still together, sleeping in the same bedroom.

St Hugh's School
25 October

Just a small note to let you know I'm going on alright here, duck. Tues and Wed we didn't have much to do, apart from a morning's route march and a little PT in the afternoon, but we've started on searchlight training today. They have moved about 50 to another camp not far away to ease the sleeping accommodation, but Ted and myself are still together.

Three of us went to see some boxing last night in the Winter Gardens between the RA [Royal Artillery] and the RASC [Royal Army Service Corps] It was a good 6d worth. Ted was on guard so he didn't come. I expect it will work round us all in time.

St Hugh's School
27 October

It soon came my turn on guard, pidge. Last night I stood 2 hrs, from 12 o'clock until 2, in the fields at the back, not a soul to talk to. My thoughts were of you, sweet, nicely tucked away in bed. Darling, this week seems the worst yet, so much further away and no chance of seeing you. Oh, if only I could tell you how much I'm missing you, love. I sure wish this lousy business somewhere when thinking of all the heartaches and longings it's causing.

Searchlights in 1940: Nan's kisses have obliterated George from the right of the picture.

St Hugh's School
[Undated]

Training's started in earnest now, love. We're not in the same squads as we were at Whatton. Ted's been put in for driving and me as a spotter, so when we have had our training, I'm afraid we shall be separated for good, worse luck. But it's been very nice to have been together. It's helped to get the worst over, darling.

Sunday seemed a long day, love, not like the days when we could get to see you. I had an eyesight and hearing test in the morning and we were on parade for 2 in the afternoon. It seemed like an ordinary weekday to me.

We've had some more kit issued, gloves, overalls, tin hat and a grand leather jerking. You can tell, love, the sergeant said it was worth around £3. But the trouble with us, dear, we haven't much room to put it. We can't leave it lying about, for the CO is hot on things like that. Nothing must be out of place when he comes round, everything has to be just so. Really, it's rotten, what with one thing and another. Not a bit of comfort in the place, darling. I'm sure it will be heaven when it's over.

We've just had a piece of pork pie, love, and it was very nice, but I shouldn't send again while we are here, for there's no knowing when we might be moved. I don't think there is much hope for a leave, sweet, but we shall have to grin and bear it, shan't we, darling, and hope for the best?

It's made things more complicated now that trouble has broken out between Greece and Italy, but it might help to shorten the war all round, love. Let's hope it has. Bombs have been dropped about here tonight, but things are quiet again now. The all clear's been sounded.

I've been to YM [YMCA] and had a game of billiards with a mate out of our room. It has passed away a quiet hour, pidge. There's no NAAFI here. All the pleasure is outside, when we have time to go, for there's always a bit of polishing to do, love.

Well, darling, I *do* miss you. I can't really think about our being parted for so long at a time. It seems awful without you, no-one to snuggle up to at night.

We've been ordered to sleep in our PT kit. They might as well tell you to sleep with nothing on. I bet the brass hats have plenty of clothes to sleep in, don't you, duck?

Well, pidge, I've let my pencil run riot tonight. I don't think I've any more news, so I will close now, dear.

From your everloving hubby

George x x x x x x x

x x x x x x

P S I wish I was bringing those myself, sweetheart.

St Hugh's School
[Undated (probably October or November)]

I'm just writing to thank you for your parcel I've just received, love, it is more than welcome. You say I haven't said anything about the food, dear. Well, I decided not to, but, as you want to know, it is giving it a good name to call it rotten. I've never seen such stuff served up before. The meat is like offal and those that serve it up are like nigger minstrels. The very smell puts you off it. All they cook is stew, or try to. We were supposed to have some for tea, but it was burnt up. The chaps just turned round and put it in the swill tub. It takes all their money to buy food from outside. Everyone will be glad to get a move from here.

St Hugh's school
[Postmark 4 November]

Well, darling, I think it has been a wonderful weekend, just to have one another for a whole night. To cuddle you up to me seemed like old times, darling. I really can't believe it's been true after such a long time parted at nights. I shall feel awfully lonely tonight, dearest, but, never mind, if ever I get leave you can bet I shall come to you, love.

I was pleased we received communion together this morning, love, for it gave me a feeling of unity. You know what I mean, sweetheart.

39

367 Btty 42nd S/L Regt R A
c/o Post Office
Potter Hanworth
Nr Lincoln
[Postmark 10 November]

I'm writing to let you know I've been moved, love, but I'm afraid the above address isn't any good, for George, the Worcester fellow, and me are being moved again on Fri. Ted is staying on at the school for a time, so I don't expect to see much of him again until this job is over, dear.

We are in huts, the wind is howling round and the lights are hurricane lamps hanging from the ceiling. But there is one advantage, we have got spring beds to lie on.

Love, I did enjoy being with you for two nights. It seemed like old times. Pictures on Sat night and a visit home Sunday afternoon.

We had to go through a gas chamber when we got back last night. Tear gas, it was, and we had to take our masks off for the last few secs. It made our eyes run, I can tell you, but it goes to prove the masks give you complete protection.

Potter Hanworth
14 November

Hardly anything to do, but not allowed to go out. It's like being in a detention camp, men moving in and out again all the time. I'm sorry I can't give you an address to write to, duck, for I *shall* welcome a letter from you, dear, but we're going tomorrow to relieve some others for their 7 days leave, so perhaps I can give you the address when I write again, pidge.

There was 21 men came here, but 13 left yesterday for another site and four of us go tomorrow. It's like playing draughts, not knowing where or when the next move is taking you.

I've done an hour's air sentry this morning. Everybody has to do an hour in their turn. Mine comes again from 1–2 in the morning. It's a lot better here for food, love, and well cooked.

Potter Hanworth
17 November

Just a line to let you know I'm alright, love, but getting
browned off with this kind of isolation stuff. I've just
come in off guard. It's about a quarter to twelve and what
a night! Simply pouring with rain and a strong wind
blowing, but still, it's kept Jerry away so far.

It was nearly 2 this morning when we got to bed, but
we slept through until ten. Darling, some of us went to
Woodhall yesterday on a clothing parade. I went for an
extra blanket and while I was there I asked about Ted. He's
still down at the school, according to what I was told. I
expect he will have a 48 hr leave this weekend.

Potter Hanworth
1 December

The officer had some bad news for us. He said men were
continually overstaying their leave, so headquarters had
decided to cut it down to 48 hrs every 80 days and 7 days
after 160, but perhaps that rule will soon fade out. I hope it
does, for it will seem years between each leave, won't it,
love?

Sweetheart, I hope Jerry don't come disturbing you
like he did Thursday night. It was rotten, but if you sit on
the sofa, I think that is the safest place, love. I wish I could
be with you, pidge, when he's around like that. I do worry
about you, darling, but I hope he keeps out of range with
his eggs.

c/o Grange Farm
Waddington
Lincolnshire
14 December

Just a few lines to let you know we have moved at last. We had quite a busy time yesterday morning, moving all the equipment. I felt about done up, for we had a night out Thurs, when Sheffield was getting it. We had as many as fifteen Jerries in our area at once, but he was up a tremendous height when he came over us. The AA [anti-aircraft] fire and bomb flashes could be seen from our site, along with the dull thuds of the explosions that we could hear.

Waddington
[Postmark 26 December]

Well, darling, I never felt the other partings so hard as the one today. You seemed so lonely and upset, dear. But never mind, it won't be long until the seven days work round and then we can have one another for a whole week, sweetheart. It has been rather a brief leave, duck, but I'm sure I enjoyed every minute of it, for I love you more than I can tell you, sweet. If only the end of this war would come so we could be together again, I'm sure we would be as happy as anybody, shouldn't we, darling?

There aren't any Jerries about tonight, love. All the fellows are in their beds, but doesn't it seem awful for them to be away from their wives and kiddies at a time like this? It seems a strange Christmas Eve, dear, the strangest I have ever spent, especially now as we ought to be together, enjoying each other's company to the full. But let us hope it's the first and last, darling.

Waddington
28 December

Well, darling, Christmas is nearly over now, but how I should have loved to be with you. I'm sure it wasn't very merry here, love. We went to church at Branston in the morning to a nice quiet service and the rest of the day most of us stopped in as there was nothing to go out for. Every man was allowed one packet of smokes and a bottle of beer, but when I went for my bottle it was missing. However, it didn't matter, love, for, as you know, I should have given it away.

How did your Christmas Day go off, pidge? I hope there wasn't any scenes as there usually is, but I expect there would be a few cases of 'one over the eight'. I was thinking about you, dear, the running about and the extra work it would mean for you, and how I should have liked to have been helping you, darling.

There haven't been any Jerries over these last two nights and all's quiet tonight up to now. Has he visited over you at all, sweet, or have you had it peaceful like us? I hope you have, love.

Well, love, it's been work again today, fetching bricks from old sites that have been abandoned and making paths on this new one, so Boxing Day has been 'just another day' for us, love.

Even the bombardier said that I was soft for getting back Christmas Eve as it would have been OK to have come back today, but it was alright to say that when I *was* here, wasn't it, love?

43

George's favourite picture of Nan, which was probably taken in 1943–44; he kept a copy in his cigarette case.

Chapter Three

'THERE'LL BE BLUEBIRDS'

Nan, 1940

[To George at Whatton-in-the-Vale]

Swan Inn
Armitage
[Postmark 26 September 1940]

Well, George, it's nearly a whole week since we parted,
but, by jove, it seems more than a month since I saw you,
love. Life seems rather dull and empty without you, but I
am trying to make the best of it, as there seems to be no
alternative.

    Now, sweetheart, a word about yourself. Try and be
as happy as you can about it and don't get disheartened. I
feel certain everything will turn out all right and don't
worry about me. I am alright now. I hope that what you
have told me in the letters is true. Oh, and by the way,
PLEASE SEND WORD IF THERE IS ANYTHING YOU
REQUIRE IN THE WAY OF MONEY OR ANYTHING ELSE.
And whatever, you do, George, please tell me the truth.

    We had some sad news from London on Tues. Uncle
Joe's son wrote and asked us if we would have his wife
Annie and her daughter Ethel and baby as Uncle Joe's
house and one of his daughters' houses had been bombed
and they were practically homeless. Isn't it terribly sad,
George? It took the letter five days to get here, so we sent a
telegram straight back to tell them to come. That was on

Tuesday and we haven't heard another word and we know the telegram got through in 20 minutes. We don't know what's happened to them since, but we think perhaps they had gone to a place where they take the homeless in and the telegram can't find them. We do hope they are safe somewhere.

I hear you have both been vaccinated and nocculated. I do hope you don't feel too bad. And by the way, what did the dentist say about your bad teeth? Have they got to come out, love?

God Bless you, love
From your everloving wife, Nan.
x x x x x

PS Be sure and do everything you are told to do and don't do anything wrong.

Swan Inn
[Late September]

Those people from London came on Monday evening and they are staying with us for a short while till it gets a bit better in London. It is a lovely baby and so unspoiled. It does seem a shame, though, for our Mary, you know and I feel it ever so for her. He is ten months old and he is fair, just like our little John would have been. [John was Mary Yardley's first child, who died soon after birth; her surviving son David was born in September 1941.] I do hope this wretched war will soon be over, then she will be able to have another. It seems awful for her with him being in the house all the time. She never picks him up. But he loves me ever so, you know, and so good he is with me. I *do* wish I had got one of my own to love.

Well, George, I am glad you decided about the house, as you say, perhaps it will be better to leave it till it is all over. It will be nice to have a home of our own actually, won't it, some day? Of our *very* own? We shall make a fuss of it, shan't we?

Mary and I went to see your Mother yesterday. We walked there and back. Felt a bit tired when we got home as we had to run home as it was getting dark. You can tell, we started from your house nearly a quarter past seven and got in home between 10 and 5 to eight. [Although only two miles, it would have been a perilous journey between Brereton and Armitage at night with the roads unlit and houses 'blacked out' under air raid precautions.]

My word, love, I have got a lot to tell you. You will be tired of reading such scribble. I must tell you I had a really lovely dream about you last night. In fact, when I woke this morning I forgot that you weren't with me and expected to see you there. It seemed so *very* real, but, never mind, it won't always be a dream, will it, darling?

Be sure and tell me the whole truth, George and *do* write to me, dear. I will say goodbye to you, hoping that God will keep you both safe and bring this awful war to a quick ending. Goodbye, dear, and God bless you both.

From your everloving wife, Nan

x x x x x x

Swan Inn
10 October

Mother has got a bad foot. She was cutting her corn and cut her little toe in mistake. I can tell you she hasn't half got a foot. She's having to poultice it as it is festering.

We haven't got any soldiers at the Towers yet, but I suppose we shall soon. It seems awful for those under canvas, doesn't it? [The Towers was a large house in the village, taken over for billeting troops.]

[To George at St Hugh's School, Woodhall Spa]

Swan Inn
25 October

We feel so worried about you both that we have sent a parcel for you to share between you, which I know will be gratefully accepted.

Mother's foot is improving a little, I think, but she gets a bit tired now. It is such a lot for her, George.

Ethel and her mother have sent you the cigarettes. I was rather surprised, love. Ethel's baby is poorly, cutting his teeth. She took him to the Doctor's this morning.

Well, love, I must tell you about my experience on Tuesday. I took it into my head to go and see your Mother on the 5 o'clock bus. I ought to have had more sense, you know. I took her birthday present. Mary and Les happened to be at Les's Mother's and they just came in time to take me back to catch the half past eight bus, as they thought. But, alas, it was so terribly foggy. Les wouldn't let me take the risk on the bus, so they both started to walk back with me.

After they had brought me home safely, I was very thankful to them both. They had only just got to your Mother and Dad and the children when the bombs dropped at Brereton. It was terrible. All the windows out at Massers and the Castle [a public house], and they dropped all round there. If they had gone back the same way as they had come with me, Les says they would have just caught it. When they got home your Dad got them down the cellar. I was worried stiff till I saw Les on Wednesday dinner time. I might tell you I shan't do that again as I should have felt responsible if anything had happened to them, but I was thankful to know they were safe. Fancy Jerry coming on such a foggy night as that. It seems to me he'll come any night after that.

Swan Inn
28 October

You don't say much about your food in your letter. I hope you aren't trying to keep it back from me as you know how it worries me. I am sending you this parcel as I think you will both be very pleased with it. Dolly has made the cake and sandwich and also sent you a packet of cigs. Ada has sent you the St Ivels cheese. Your Mother is sending you a parcel this week as well, so you will write and let us know if you receive them, won't you?

Dad is on the ARP [air raid precautions] this afternoon and we are in a bit of a muddle. Oh, George, that little baby is so poorly. You would feel ever so sorry for him, and that girl is so unkind. She shook him awful in bed the other night because he kept her awake. Mother would insist on her to take him to the Doctor's yesterday, even if it was Sunday. He doesn't know what to think as his little ear is so bad it might lead to anything, he says. But the Doctor is the same opinion as me, he hasn't half enough clothes on, poor little chap. We do wish they would go back as she is so cattish with us. It does seem a shame for Mother.

I am pleased to say I am feeling better, but we don't have much time for rest with these people here. We don't think they will stop much longer when the baby gets better.

Swan Inn
30 October

I am writing this letter to you, love, at Mary's. There has been a few sharp words at home, so we have decided to come down here, as we thought it was best and, in any case, Mary would have done, as there are quite a few noseyparkers want to know where she is staying at and does she want to let her house.

The words were because we were not able to clean the kitchen up on Monday as those people were on top of the hearth all the time and Mother said we did not want to do it, you see. It was very unkind, I thought, after all we are having to contend with and you being away too. But Dolly has been down and she seems quite upset about Mother as her foot seems so painful.

I do wish those people never had come as it is all through them. It seems everyone is against us, George, but never mind, there is always one who knows and there always comes a day of reckoning.

When I went to your Mam's on Sunday, my mind went back to those happy days when we used to walk in the brisk frost on Sunday afternoons. I felt ever so upset about it and sad too. I sometimes wonder if they will ever come back, dear. I felt so lonely all on my own.

PS Don't forget to do everything as you ought to do and don't cause me any worry, love.

[From George's mother]

Red Brook Lane
[November 1940]

We have had a few quiet nights. It was awful on Friday, they were backward and forward all night. I believe Brum is as bad as Coventry. There were 9 bombs dropped at Colton on Friday night. We did not go to bed. I went after your Dad had gone to work on Saturday morning.

[From Nan]

Swan Inn
25 November

Please don't think me ungrateful for not writing straight back to you, love, but I really waited to see if you came home this weekend. Alas, I waited in vain, but never mind, love, perhaps it won't be long before I see you. I wasn't the only one who was disappointed as Ted never came again this weekend.

It is very quiet everywhere, all the same, I have got a sad bit of news to tell you. You know Harry Sharratt's little boy, John? Well, on Friday he strayed down to the brook and, with it being flooded, the water must have attracted him and the poor little chap fell in and got drowned.

Isn't it terrible for them, George? He must have been in the water about 3 hours, as they missed him just before twelve. When they dragged for him it was about half past three when they got him out. It was Harry himself that actually found him. They are nearly off their heads about it as he was so wanted, you know.

The soldiers have all gone. The sergeant took me Dad to a boxing tournament the night before they went, up at the camp. Real good performance, I believe. Jimmy Wilde's son, Jack London and Ernie Roderick and one or two more. He thoroughly enjoyed it, he said. But after the boxing they did some of that all in wrestling. He says it was terrible the things they did. Pulling one another's hair and ears. He says it was awful, never wants to go again.

[From George's mother]

Red Brook Lane
25 November

We had bombs dropped on Tuesday in the village. One
dropped in the Castle garden. It has done some damage to
the houses, Astbury's and Massers, and broke windows on
the other side of the road. One dropped over Crosses
bridge. It fetched the bedroom ceiling in at one house on
the canalside and broke a lot of windows at the
bungalows. And there was one at the five arches, but
no-one was hurt, thank God. We all went to the cellar. I
think the balloon barrage was too strong for them and
they dropped the bombs anywhere. All's well that ends
well.

[From Nan]

Swan Inn
[Early December]

We have been nearly full in the bar this morning. The
sergeants have come in advance of the troops. They are
coming on Wednesday, so I suppose we shall be packed
out once again. The sergeants told my Dad 80 of them are
'gentlemen's sons' from London, so I reckon we shall be
having a bit of 'that posh London twang' that I am so fond
of hearing.
    I went to Church yesterday afternoon, but I'm afraid
people forget there is such a place. You would think they
would go more at these awful times, never mind about
disliking the Rector.

Swan Inn
6 December

I am just having a few minutes on my own upstairs to
write this letter to you, love, as it is like a bedlam
downstairs. Brian is so naughty and Ethel is so nasty.

I have been up early with Mary this morning and
since Ethel has got up she hasn't done a tap of work. It is
nearly unbearable, George. Her husband is coming
tomorrow and Mother and Dad are seriously thinking of
asking him to take her back with him. It is beginning to
tell on Mother, as she is not able to have her five minutes
rest in comfort. She looks ever so worn out.

Swan Inn
10 December

Ethel and George have just gone to the station. He has
been here since Saturday, but mother had quite a talk with
them both while we were out last night. She told them
quite plain that if he wanted her to stop here she would
have to be prepared to do a bit of work.

By the way, I must tell you, Ethel and I had a row on
Saturday morning. I gave her a good telling off about
picking on people. I trembled like a leaf, but I told her it
was my home when all's said and done. I bet she never
likes me any more. She cried with temper. You can see
there isn't any love lost, is there?

Swan Inn
18 December

Christmas won't mean anything to me this year without
the one who means so much to me. I don't think I'll ever
get used to this life without you as it seems so lonely, dear.
I do so hope and pray it will soon come to an end and
peace be restored once more. It will seem like another
world.

I do hope you will be alright as regards food at this
new place and you won't be too lonely, as it will be so
monotonous for you. By the way, don't wear your knitted

socks too long and don't you wash them. Wear your ones out of the army and I will wash the knitted ones if you bring them.

The soldiers will be here tomorrow, so I expect we shall be on the trot again.

[To George at Grange Farm, Waddington (Christmas card enclosed)]

Swan Inn
20 December

Just a small letter to you, hoping you are alright. This is my third letter to you this week and I haven't received one since Monday, which was wrote on Saturday. I am beginning to wonder whether there is such a person still as 'Mrs Scragg Junior', or are your letters going elsewhere?

They aren't very nice soldiers which have come this time. Most of them are in civvies, new recruits, just come from home on Wednesday to be trained at the Towers. They didn't seem to like the idea of straw beds, just coming from home. But they seem regular snobs, picking you up over the least thing and finding faults.

Darling, it will soon be Christmas but, alas, what a Christmas this year it will be for everyone. Darling, I am so sorry we shall be apart from each other for that Wonderful Day, so I am sending you this Christmas card, just for you, to remember me. I think the words are so nice George, and I am sending it to you, love, not to wish you a Merry and a Happy Xmas, because I know only too well, dear, it can't be that. But because I thought it would be just a little reminder of me and of the happy days we spent together and I hope we shall live to spend some more, I am sure I am sending it to you with my very best love.

[From George's mother]

Red Brook Lane
22 December

We killed the pig yesterday. It was just 10 score. Nan has not been today. It is so soon dark and Jerry has been busy this last 3 nights. He dropped 4 bombs last night round by the Trent Valley. I thought our time had come. It was half past 3 before we went to bed and half past 1 on Friday and it looks like being late again. Dear son, I hope you do not get him much.

[From Nan]

Swan Inn
23 December

Well, George, Mary had a nice surprise after all. She had a letter yesterday morning to say Ted was coming, but he didn't say for how long. She intended to go to Lichfield with Nora and myself, but after she got her letter she naturally cancelled it. Anyhow, Nora and Heather and myself went and Jack came after on his bicycle. While we were in Lichfield there was a great big craner belonging to the army going through the streets and Jack said Ted was in it, he felt sure. It stopped right at the top of the street and we were at the bottom, so, of course, Jack ran his hardest to see. And, George, it actually was Ted. It would have been nice, after all, if Mary had come with us, but anyhow he stopped and bought her a lovely string of pearls for her Christmas present.

Swan Inn
30 December

Well, dear, I must tell you it seems like living in a whirlwind here. Of all the years we have been at the Swan, my Dad says we have never experienced such a busy Christmas. Ted came in very useful, I can tell you.

You can tell what it's been like, we had sold out of pint beers on Xmas night alone. I really wonder how I have kept on my legs every night from about half past six till ten turned. I have never sold so much port and cocktails before. It took three of us down the smoke room alone Xmas and Boxing night. We were packed out again last night. I can't tell I have any legs sometimes. And yesterday dinner was the same.

Well, I thought I must have a breather yesterday, so I went to church in the afternoon. It was a lovely Carol Service. All the little choir boys singing and reading the lessons. I did enjoy it. It was quite a change to be able to sit for an hour.

I went to the eleven o'clock Communion Service on Christmas Day. I though it looked awful when about 4 soldiers and the officer went up to the altar out of about 35 to 50 men. You can soon pick them out. They are a sarky lot to serve, I can tell you.

There is a Corporal here, about the only decent one to serve out of them. He only comes from Uttoxeter. It is quite handy for him, isn't it? He told us he went home yesterday and he was just in time for tea. He said he had a married brother killed at Dunkirk, only 29 he said he was.

He doesn't half carry on about these silly girls going after these soldiers here. He says there's only about two out of them that aren't married men. Oh, George, it's shocking the carrying on in here. They pull my leg about you being the same, but I don't think you'll be tempted, will you? I do trust you, darling, and I'm sure I love you too much to do anything on you. I *do* hope it will soon end and we can be together again. Look after yourself, George, and keep warm.

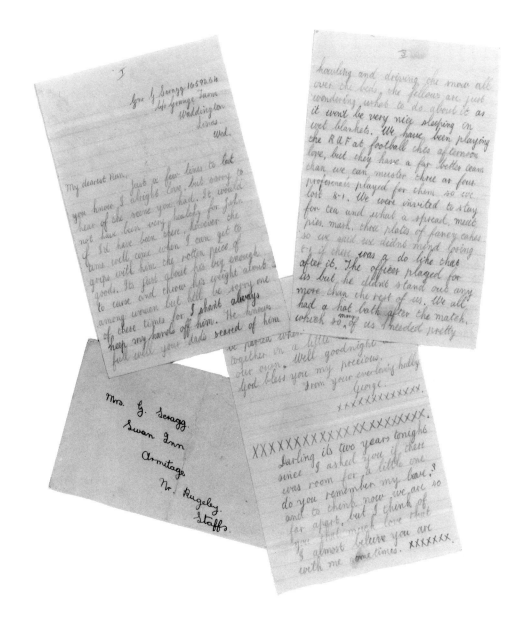

Gnr G Scragg 16592.64
6/o Grange Farm
Waddington
Lincs.
Wed.

My dearest Nan,
           Just a few lines to let
you know I alright love, but sorry to
hear of the scare you had. It would
not have been very healthy for John
if I'd have been there, however the
time will come when I can get to
grips with him the rotten piece of
goods. I's fed about his big enough
to cure and throw his weight about
among women but he'll be sorry one
of these times for I shan't always
keep my hands off him. He knows
full well your dads scared of him.

3

howling and driving the snow all
over the beds, the fellows are just
wondering what to do about it as
it wont be very nice sleeping in
wet blankets. We have been playing
the R.A.F at football this afternoon
love, but they have a far better team
than we can muster three or four
professionals played for them so we
lost 8-1. We were invited to stay
for tea and what a spread, meat
pies, mash, choc plates of fancy cakes
so we said we didns mind losing
or if there was a do like that
after it. The officer played for
us but he didns stand out any
more than the rest of us. We all
had a hot bath after the match,
which so many of us needed pretty

... parza when
together on a little
our own.
          Well goodnight
God bless you my precious,
          From your ever-loving hubby
                    George.
          xxxxxxxxxx.

xxxxxxxxxxxxxxxxxxxxxx.
darling its two years tonight
since I asked you if there
was room for a little one,
do you remember my love,?
and to think now we are so
far apart, but I think of
you that much love that
I almost believe you are
with me sometimes. xxxxxxx.

Mrs. G. Scragg.
Swan Inn
Armitage
Nr. Rugeley.
Staffs.

Chapter Four

'KISS ME GOODNIGHT, SERGEANT-MAJOR'

George, 1941

Waddington
31 December 1940

Dearest Nan

Just a few lines, sweetheart, to wish you health and happiness in the coming year. Darling, I only hope that next New Year's we will find the peoples all at peace and everybody united again. It seems a rather odd way of spending it here, as I'm on the duty team tonight, and can't go out for just a drink. Do you remember, love, the New Year's Eves of the past, when we were together and everyone making merry? Let's hope they will come again, so that they will *mean* something to us all.

Waddington
5 January

I hardly know how to begin this letter, as I haven't heard from you since I came back, a fortnight this coming Tuesday. What is the matter, love? Is there anything the matter at home, or are your letters going astray? I'm sure I don't know what to think. I am very anxious and disappointed about it, darling. Can't just get it out of my mind, nearly worried stiff, but perhaps you can explain matters when you do write. I can't seem to concentrate on anything I do and I'm sure I don't want to go out. I feel proper down, love. I hope there is nothing the matter with you and no trouble at home, dear, but I can't make heads or tails of it all.

Well, darling, I can't write any more so will close now.

Do, please, write, love, for you are all the world to me.

Waddington
7 January

Darling, whatever is the matter with you? Is there anything wrong, love? I wish you would write to me, for I am at my wits end wondering what has come over you. It's nearly a fortnight since I left you and I've wrote about six times without reply. There isn't a more disappointed man in the whole army than me at the present moment. I've asked sergeant for a daylight leave to come and see what the trouble is. If I don't get it, I shall take it on my own, for the suspense is awful. Well, darling, please let me know *what* is the matter, for I'm sick at heart worrying.

Waddington
10 January

I got back alright, but it was the worst journey ever. It was twelve o'clock before I got in. However, it was OK. I was in Newark at 10 to 9, but it was impossible to get a lift, nobody would stop, so I started to walk it. I should think I did about 8 miles before an army lorry pulled up and took me to Lincoln. I was never more grateful for a lift in my life, darling, for I was about all in. In fact, I thought about dossing in a haystack until morning. I started trudging towards Waddington, when a car pulled up and brought me to the site.

Darling, there was three of your letters arrived by this morning's post and the one from your mam, the registered one, came this morning. I think they had been to the drome. However, they had not been opened.

I can't tell you how thankful I was to see you alright.

It was a very anxious time this last week. I feel a new man
now, knowing everything is alright with you, love.

Darling, I *do* love you and you need never be afraid of
me doing anything wrong, for you are all and everything
to me, dearest. Roll on next Friday, a week tomorrow.

Waddington
13 January

Did Jerry visit you last night, dear? He came over here, but
it was Grantham that had the bombs, and according to one
of the bricklayers who comes from there, about twenty
were killed and quite a number injured during the raid.
Isn't it a shame, love, for the innocent women and children?

Waddington
26 January

Darling, I've got back safely after a rotten journey,
waiting on every station.

How nice of you to come to the station with me,
darling, and give a smile to see me off. I'm sure it was very
plucky of you to smile under the circumstances, and I shall
always remember it, darling, for it cheered me up no end.
I really can't tell you how much I enjoyed my leave with
you, dearest, but I'm sure it was seven days of heaven.

Goodnight, my love, and may God Bless you. Oh, to
be with you to wish it to you, dear. It will be a lonely
George who gets into bed tonight.

Waddington
27 January

I'm alright, love, but can't settle down to it properly as
yet. I *do* miss you, sweetheart, after having you for a
week. It's begun to snow again, proper winter weather, so
do take care of yourself, won't you, pidge? The snow
plough is still clearing the roads here, for it's been very
bad. The chaps had to go and bring the rations in from the
lorry, which got stuck.

Love, I shall be glad when the other fellows come back to ease the guard, for it's pretty stiff, anything up to seven hours in twenty-four and on duty team every night.

Darling, don't let those soldiers rag you. They seem to enjoy tormenting you, but take no notice, it's only their ignorance. Sweetheart, I shall be pleased when it's all over and I can take you away from that kind of life. It's not for you, my precious.

Waddington
[End January]

Well, pidge, it's been all rain here these last two days, but it didn't stop the 'blitz', as the officer calls it, on the digging. It's been five o'clock before we could knock off at nights, working in the pouring rain. Do you know what he did yesterday? He went and asked the farmer for the horse and cart to fetch some turfs, but the farmer told him that even horses wanted a rest sometimes, so he couldn't have it. I'm sure he would work us till we drop, carting turfs, digging and putting down concrete slabs.

Waddington
28 January

We had the King and Queen visiting the drome yesterday to decorate some of the airmen. I was on guard when they came back, so I gave them the 'present arms'. Both waved and smiled. They were escorted by four other cars and while they were at the drome fighter planes patrolled the whole of the time. Well, love, it's the first time I've seen them, but I wished you could have done, as you have always said you would like to.

Waddington
[Early February]

I wasn't on the duty team last night, but during rouser the sergeant had me out with a rifle in case anything happened. I think he's got the wind up over an invasion. But I asked

the officer if it was necessary for me to be out. He said it
wasn't, so I came in and went to bed.

Did Jerry come over your way, love, for he was
pretty close here about half past four this morning, nearly
shaking us out of bed. I thought he'd got the drome, but
they were just the other side, thank the Lord. They are just
turning out on rouser, but I can't hear any planes yet.

The sergeant had us scrubbing out the huts yesterday.
Said they were filthy. And while we were on the job a
report came through from headquarters that ours was the
cleanest site in the troop, so you can tell what he's like.

Waddington
[Early February]

One of our bombardiers has thrown in his stripes this
week, but he is still here as a gunner like the rest of us. It
appears that he was guard commander one night at Battery
HQ when one of the guards threw his rifle in and did a
bunk. The blame was put on the bombardier, but how
was he to know that it had happened, for he only goes out
with the fresh guard every two hours. However, they said
something to him which he resented, so he handed in his
stripes. Too bad, for he's a good sort.

Waddington
[Early February]

Last night's team was out from half past six until twelve,
just about froze when they came in, poor devils, and that
was after an afternoon's digging. I don't think there is a
worse mob in the British army than searchlights, for it's
impossible to say you've done.

Darling, it's two years tonight since I asked you if
there was room for a little one. Do you remember, my
love? And to think now we are so far apart. But I think of
you so much, love, that I almost believe you are with me
sometimes.

Waddington
16 February

We *did* have a night last night, pidge, in and out of bed
from half past seven until the same time this morning.
Towards the finish, I didn't know whether I was coming
or going, absolutely beat. We were only allowed in bed
until ten and I've been digging all day, but I'm not on duty
tonight, thank the Lord, so I can have a rest, apart from
guard from 12–2.

Daylight leave has been stopped here until all the
digging is completed, so there will be no more half days
off just yet. We seem to have a lot more men coming here
now. I should think there is nearly 40, but some are
without beds.

The OC [Officer Commanding] has been round
today and he seems quite pleased with everything. The
sergeant who is so well-liked, I don't think, has gone on
forty-eight hrs leave, so we shan't be pestered with him
for a couple of days. He's proper windy and we don't half
play him up, but he can't see it.

Waddington
[Early March]

We've been into Woodhall again today and I saw some of
Ted's mates, so I told them to remember me to him.

The new sergeant went with us and we called in the
WVS for a cup of tea and a sandwich and he paid for all the
tea. He's a grand chap to get along with. The officer
wanted him to work us till ½ past 4, but he told him he
wasn't in the habit of breaking his promises to the men, so
it stayed as it was.

St Hugh's School
Woodhall Spa
1 May [on a course]

Just a few lines to let you know I got back alright but it
was about ½ past 11. I didn't start from Burton till 3
o'clock on the bus and I travelled by bus to Saxendale
crossroads, as all the cars seemed to be full up. Well, dear,
I got to Lincoln a bit at a time, arriving there about 10 to 7,
too late for the bus, so went to the station to enquire about
the train. There was one leaving for Woodhall at 10-15, so
I went to the N A A F I and then to the pictures to pass
away the time. There wasn't any time to write last night,
love, so you will excuse me, won't you?
    I forgot to tell you, Sam Hollins had the night in
Derby, didn't get home to Stoke till 11. His wife asked
him how long he'd come for. He said, 'a wash and shave
and I'm off back.' Five were missing on the first parade.

Whatton-in-the-Vale
14 May

We've had a quiet time at night since Sun, no Jerries about.
The officer went to Waddington yesterday. I believe he's
about flattened the village out. The quaint old church has
gone and there is only about three houses not affected.
Potter's site had a close shave, six 500 lbs bombs only
about 15 yards off the lights, so according to that, love, we
should have had a rough time if we had still been there.
    The N A A F I only allow 5 fags per man now, love, I
can see a lot finishing smoking altogether.

Whatton-in-the-Vale
18 May

We wash and stand by our beds just before tea for the M O
to examine us, as there is some cases of scabies in camp.
One of our room has been sent to hospital, but it's not
certain whether he's got them or not. What a sight,
though, thirty-odd men in their birthday suits.

63

Waddington
6 June

I don't think I've mentioned it before, love, but we've got
a sergeant major stopping with us at present, not a bad
sort, taking him on the whole, but we could manage
nicely without him. He came round last night for
volunteers, either for parachutists or commandants
[sic – probably commandos], fellows who sail near the
French coast, swim ashore, do as much damage as possible
and swim back.

    I told him I might be fed up with the army, but didn't
want to commit suicide just yet. One young chap had his
name put down for the parachutists. I think he must be
tired of living, don't you, love?

Waddington
[Mid June]

We've been to Potter today training. Everyone is fed up
with it. We are just like tin soldiers, just here to be played
with. I wish the ATS, would come out to man the lights,
we might stand a chance of being transferred into *the army*,
love.

    I think we've got the lousiest set of NCOs that we
have ever had. The SM has turned out a beauty. He took
one chap into Battery today on a charge, a happening that
anyone else would have let go by. The chap had to report
sick to Woodhall, but instead of waiting for transport
back, he hitch-hiked it, which made him rather late.
Anyway, love, he's got 14 days' pay stopped and 7 days
CB [confined to barracks], so I think he's had it pretty
thick.

Waddington
[Mid June]

We had a good lift from Saxendale right into Lincoln with
a naval officer and his wife. It was a grand car, doing 60
most of the way, so we soon covered the distance, pidge.
He said he was going to Grimsby as his leave was up

tomorrow. He'd had 4 days. A month ago, he was in New York, bringing back a cargo of USA planes. He seemed a grand sort of a fellow.

Waddington
21 June

We are getting plenty of sunshine, just working in shorts and pumps, so we shall be browned off proper if it keeps like this for long.

    We are busy making camouflage netting to put on the equipment during the daytime so Jerry won't be able to pick us out. But it's all got to be taken off at nights, so that's extra work for us, I suppose. I'm on air sentry as I write this, in the gunpit. It's all sentry and guard these days, only 11 men to do it.

Waddington
23 June

I've been listening to Mr Churchill's speech and I think if Russia can stand up to him, Hitler, the war will be over by Christmas. I think the little runt has put his head into the noose good and proper this time, for, in my opinion, America won't be long before she is in it up to the neck.

    I suppose you were listening to it, love. Don't you think the news that followed was heartening as well? 27 down for 1 of ours. [This probably refers to the almost nightly 'scores' of German and British planes shot down which were broadcast at this time as the battle for air supremacy began to escalate.] Darling, I don't think we shall be apart much longer, if the Lord keeps us safe to the end.

Waddington
20 July

Love, we are all having to stay in this weekend as there are
some invasion manoeuvres on with the Home Guard
round here. We'll have to wear tin hats everywhere we go
to distinguish us from the 'enemy' who are wearing forage
caps. The chaps are wishing it somewhere, I can tell you.
We are all issued with leather equipment, belts, pouches,
etc., strapped up like horses now.

Waddington
23 July

One of our bombers crashed on Lincoln High School close
to the cathedral, setting fire to it. I heard the crash and
reported it to BHQ and should have gone to it, only they
said there would be plenty of soldiers to guard it. Don't it
seem rotten luck, getting back here after facing AA fire
over Germany, to crash on the doorstep?

Waddington
29 July

Lincoln seems to be in luck's way with crashes. Two
collided over there yesterday teatime, Spitfires, they were.
Eight people were killed, but one of the pilots bailed out
and saved himself from almost certain death. I don't think
it's a very safe spot to be in just lately, do you, love?
    We didn't have any planes over last night. It's a treat
to have a good night's sleep, you feel more like doing
things when you get up.

Waddington
31 July

There were only three people killed in that crash I told you
about, love, not 9 as I was told at first. I have put a cutting
of it in the letter.

Waddington
2 August

I've just come back from guarding still another crash
between here and Lincoln, a bomber just being tested. It's
not a very nice job, love, bits of the men lying around.
There were four in it, one a Rhodesian who just went up
for the trip, you know, love, like us from here wanted to.
All were killed and burnt. I was glad when the airforce
sent their own guard. The smell was awful. Don't there
seem to be some crashes round here just lately? One
crashed 4 or 5 miles up the road Wed night, but the crew
jumped for it and escaped injury. They were lucky, for it
was loaded up with bombs.

Waddington
3 September

Thank you, darling, for remembering my birthday. I
should have been disappointed if I hadn't heard from you,
love.
        Two planes were in the crash on Sun, love. It appears
that a fighter was practising diving attacks on bombers
and, through an error of judgment, cut this bomber's tail
clean off. Both caught fire and all were killed outright.
Don't it seem dreadful, love, getting killed in this country,
when they have probably been over Germany many
times?

Waddington
26 September

The officer has gone from here and we've a fresh sergeant,
love, who is rather mustard. I've been cleaning all the
chaps' greatcoats buttons for quite a while now and, bless
me, if he didn't put me on spud bashing because mine
wasn't up to scratch today! It's a good one, don't you
think, love?
        We haven't heard when we are moving yet, love. I
wish we weren't, really, as it's so convenient here.

Potter Hanworth
[Mid December]

What do you think of Japan and America starting war on
each other? War is like fire, it does spread, love. I hope that
it will shorten it, but, in my opinion, it won't help us any,
for we shan't be able to have so much from them. Russia
seems to be hitting back hard. I hope they can keep it up.

Potter Hanworth
26 December

Well, Darling, that's another Christmas Day gone and we
are still away from each other, but I think it's the last one
to be parted, love.

Dearest, I hope you had a quiet time and enjoyed
yourself, which, I suppose, you would if the beer didn't

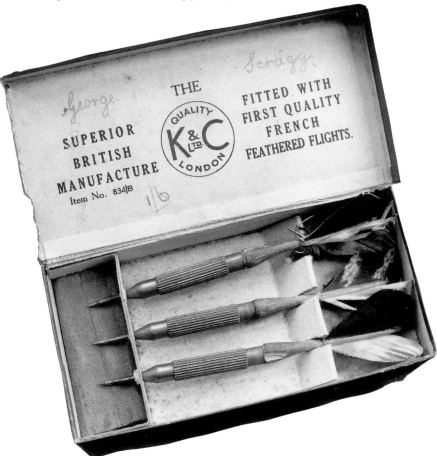

come. We had a grand time here, all we could wish for,
apart from being at home, where we all would rather have
been.

No-one in the army had more than we for dinner,
port, two fowl, roast spuds, sprouts and pudding. The tea
at the farm was excellent, home cured boiled ham and
tongue, salad, trifle, Xmas cake and fancy cakes. In fact,
love, it was nothing like wartime food we had yesterday. I
only wish everyone was able to have the same.

We had just finished tea when we had to go out for air
co-operation. Fancy, love, Christmas night and they
couldn't leave us alone. We were out for an hour and a
half. We fixed the phone down to the farm so it only
meant one man being up there on guard. We did an hour
each, so no-one was away from the party long.

Some went to church in the morning. I should have
liked to have gone, love, but I was on guard from 10–12.
Perhaps it was best, for they came back worse for drink,
love.

My word, pidge, they didn't half mop some ale.
About ten dozen bottles, besides that sherry and other
wine at the farm. I had four bottles of stout and was about
the only sober one amongst them.

The sergeant was absolutely out. He didn't get up till
nearly 11. Still, we stuck in bed up to ½ past 9 and there
hadn't been a guard on all night, but it's passed off OK
and I suppose we shall make up for it at some future date.

George attached a brooch to the front of this card to Nan.

Chapter Five

'ROLL OUT THE BARREL'

Nan, 1941

Swan Inn
1 January

Well, dear, Xmas is over and I am very thankful, I can tell you. It is quietening down a bit now. Goodness me, if things were as busy as that all the time, there wouldn't be very much left of me when you come home for your seven days leave. I shall certainly take a week off that week as I think I will deserve it.

We haven't been troubled with Jerry for over a week now. It seems lovely at night, I can tell you, with no planes overhead. You can get a good night's sleep. I *do* worry about you when they are about.

What about London, though, George? Not satisfied with bombing it, starting to burn it down now. Oh, what awful happenings. You really can't imagine such wicked things going on, can you, love?

We weren't very busy last night, as they let the soldiers in at the New Year's Ball at the club. Doesn't it seem awful, George, nearly all married men and going out with these young girls about here? People try to sneer at me and say I don't know what you are doing while you are away. But I don't take any notice of them because I *do* trust you, love, to remember those vows you made when we were married.

Ada says there is a young girl at Brereton expecting

and it's one of those last lot of soldiers that came, dragoon guards. She is only 16 and they can't trace which soldier it was. Before long it will be happening here, I'm afraid. The carrying on is simply shocking. They go about asking for trouble.

[From Nan's mother]

Swan Inn
1 January

Well, dear George, I hope you won't be too disappointed over the turkey, but you will have to have a word about it when you come home with the Dad. He only went down the cellar and ate what I had put on one side, so, of course, he has been eating turkey ever since. I don't know what ever made him do it, but he must have had a bit each time he went down to ease the pegs, which was pretty often. I could have dropped when I went down to fetch it up and found it had gone. But never mind, I will make it up when you come home, if not before.

[From Nan]

Swan Inn
6 January

We weren't so busy these nights. I aren't sorry, either. They are talking of cutting the beer down as we can't get all our bottle stuff now, so I don't know what will happen. We have no Woodbines, chocs or biscuits or cider, so you can tell things are getting short a bit.

Swan Inn
8 January

The food office won't grant Mother a permit to cut the soldiers any bread and cheese. We have to keep refusing them all the time. I think they ought to have done, really, but they have finished issuing them.

We had the sirens last night, but it soon went all clear again.

[Registered letter]

Swan Inn
9 January

I received another letter from you this morning and you still say you haven't received any letters from me. Well, George, it just puzzles me where they are going to. I sent you four nice letters last week and another one yesterday and you haven't received one yet.

Well, dear, I thought of sending you a telegram, but Miss Morecroft [the postmistress] said if I sent a registered letter they would have to let you have it as you would have to sign for it.

Don't worry about me. I'm alright, but how you must be feeling about it, not having a letter from me. Please don't blame me in any way, as I'm sure it is a pleasure to write to you, love, with you being so far away from me. If I was you, I should enquire at your end, as it seems so strange not receiving one of them even.

Please don't get the idea I don't think about you, because I am so looking forward to a week on Friday, darling, when I shall have you for a whole week.

Swan Inn
14 January

Dear, I think this will be the last letter till you come home for your 7 days leave. I am so looking forward to Friday, love. I am going to press your suit this afternoon and I will get your things well aired.

I expect it will seem very nice to have a week's rest again and a game or two of solo, love. I shall never grumble about the cards and your few pleasures anymore. After this lot is over, all being well, if we are spared to each other, we will spend the rest of our life in a happier way than these last two years of our young married life.

Swan Inn
30 January

What a nice occasion for you to see the King and Queen. I am sure you must have felt rather important being the lucky one to be on guard at the time. I wish I could see them, as you know how I have always wanted to.

The sergeants told my Dad the other night that they have stood up to the head ones about not having anything to eat after 4 o'clock and so they have given them permission to have two eggs and chips and bread for sixpence for supper. You can tell how hungry they must have been, the sergeants stood and ate dry bread in our bar on Sunday night. I did feel sorry for them. One of them told me he'd fight for it before he'd go without.

Swan Inn
[End January]

First of all I must tell you that Ethel and George and little Brian went back this morning on the 8 o'clock train. He has taken her to stay with a fireman's wife at Essex, out of London. When he came on Thursday and told us he had come to take her back I could have thrown my hat into the air.

Swan Inn
[Early February]

Oh, George, they have had those poor soldiers out there all day drilling them. They even have to put their rifles against our walls. There has been two officers, two regimental sergeant majors, about three sergeants and corporals as well.

The people are crying shame on them round here. It looks awful, straight in front of a public house as well. They are having a big parade out here tomorrow. The Colonel is coming to inspect them, so you can guess what it will be like out there tomorrow. We can't shake our mats out of the top room, or anything. If they can't do it right they have them doing it one by one till they do it properly. It is shocking.

Swan Inn
[Early February]

The soldiers had their farewell dance last night, I believe. They are going next week. I believe there are some carryings on. There's a Mrs Armstrong lives up at the Warings Estate, wife of a signalman. The war's broke their home up alright. She has gone off with the sergeant of the advance party last Tuesday. Isn't it shocking, George?

Well, worse than that, a fortnight last Sunday night, M.M. and C.M. were with two soldiers in the Plum Pudding. One was that Alfonso, as they call him, the other has a moustache. Well, it appears they often go down there. Mr Ramsay that keeps the Pudding thought that as there was such a good fire he wouldn't waste the light in the big room, so he left them all four in there.

George, you will be astounded at what I have got to tell you. A Mr and Mrs Edwards came in very quickly and quietly so, of course, he switched the light on rather sharp, and what a scene met his eyes. They were all four on the floor, George, absolutely right on the job. That Alfonso had nothing on up to his waist.

I really don't know what Armitage is coming to. It's perfectly true, George, it's in everybody's mouth. Even the kids have got it at school and they own up to it. Mr Ramsay said he didn't have much trade, but he wasn't going to allow that sort of thing. I think it's right-down filthy, George. Fancy, in a public house above all places.

Swan Inn
8 February

I have just been to the churchyard with Mary for a little blow. As we were there it was about a quarter to four and my mind went back two years this afternoon. Think of it, love. As I looked at the time, I said to Mary, 'It's just about two years now and we were just married. If only this awful war would end and we were together again.'

The food situation is getting awful. There isn't any cheese round here and they can't get lots of other things besides. The cigarettes are very scarce, but I'm not going to lose any of those I've saved for you.

75

Swan Inn
[Mid February]

A terrible tragedy has occurred at Armitage this weekend.
You know young Muriel Jones from down the Old Road?
Well, it appears she has been friendly with a corporal from
up at the Towers. Her Dad and Mum were very worried
about it, George, as, you see, he was a married man. Well,
anyhow, they forbid her to go with him, naturally, and
Phyllis got on to her as well. But, alas, it didn't stop her.
She has been missing from Saturday night at seven and
they couldn't find her up to Sunday morning.

   Anyhow, they decided to drag the canal for her as
they had found her bicycle she had been riding close by the
milking bank bridge. Well, they found her body just
behind the church in the canal. Oh, George, I think it's
terrible and only fifteen too, all her life in front of her.

Swan Inn
27 February

It seemed awful on Sunday without you, George, and
when bedtime came, it was worse still. I seemed so lonely,
getting into bed on my own. In fact, I'll tell you frankly I
cried myself to sleep. I couldn't stop the tears coming,
they just had to come. I expect it was worse, as Mary is
usually there after you've gone back. Well, I consoled
myself as best I could. I kissed your pillow many a time
over, darling.

Swan Inn
6 March

George, you will never stop laughing when I tell you that
Mr Gallimore is going to be a Daddy at the age of 63. I
believe she had no idea she was like that as she is just at that
funny stage of life. The Doctor came to see her on Sunday
and he examined her and turned round and told her she
was six months gone. Fancy, George, and not knowing
and a nurse, too, at that. The folks aren't half smiling
about it, I can tell you. Can you imagine Victor pushing
the pram?
    The soldiers are having their finale at the Swan
tonight, so you can bet we shall be packed out. They are
paying them out tonight so I expect they will make it fly a
bit.

    PS Mary can't get over Mrs Gallimore and Victor.
She says the sirens must have disturbed them.

Swan Inn
12 March

My word, George, we haven't had Jerry for a long time,
but, by jove, we had him last night alright. I never heard
such bombs before. He dropped about 10 at Kings
Bromley and never hurt anyone. Talk about shake the
house. Frank said it nearly shook the crocks out of their
cupboards. The people seem to think he followed the 9
o'clock train up the line. Others think he was after Fradley
[airfield].

Swan Inn
7 April

Dear, I felt very lonely after you had gone. I don't think I
have ever felt it so much, but I didn't let you see I was
down. When I went to bed I just cried and cried myself to
sleep.
    It seems the war is getting worse now he has made his
attack on the Balkans. Fancy starting bombing them

already. What a shame for these small countries and little valiant Greece having to face an army like theirs.

I am surprised to hear about Frank Lowe and the boys going voluntary like that. Whatever happens, George, don't you go and volunteer, as I am worried in case you *have* to go.

Swan Inn
10 April

Yesterday Mary and I went for a little walk and we both said we ought to be going in to get a nice tea for you both. Instead, it's the same old routine, nothing to go in for.

I *love* to go for my communion lately. It's nice to be quiet for half an hour sometimes, although it makes you feel sad when you think of the world in such a terrible position. I shall never get used to living without you, love, as I am sure when you love one another it makes all the difference.

Swan Inn
[May]

Love, you won't half laugh when I tell you what I dreamt last night. I was with another chap in bed and I was going to have a baby by him. Honest, I never had a dream that seemed so real. I can tell you I was glad I woke up and found it was only a dream. You would have had something to say about it, wouldn't you, love?

It is a lovely day today. The sun is getting quite warm towards afternoon. But what a pity this awful bombing is going on. It doesn't seem human to keep killing the civil population off like this. The poor women and children must be suffering agonies in these big towns. Night after night like this.

Swan Inn
[May]

We had Jerry knocking about rather a lot last night. It was
my Dad's night out and we lay and listened to the planes
going over. He wasn't half low, too. We are all so very
tired with lying awake all night. We overslept this
morning and it was a quarter past eight when I woke up,
but the work's been done just the same.

Mary and Nan on holiday.

Swan Inn
25 May

I have cooked the dinner today and I don't think you
would have minded eating it, darling, although they
always say, 'Our Nan can't do this and our Nan can't do
that.' I am sure I shall suit you, George, if ever we have the
chance to live together, love.

Swan Inn
3 June

We are busy at home, still cleaning out. We are going to
whitewash the lavatory and pantry this week, all being
well.
    The brewery men told us on Saturday they are going
to start and ration the beer in a fortnight's time, so, if they
do,. we shall try and work it so we close on a Sunday. It
will be much nicer for us, won't it, dear?
    My word, what's it coming to, love, rationing for
clothes? It won't make any difference to me, though, as
you know I'm always very careful and mend them all up.

[From George's mother]

Red Brook Lane
[June]

Dear Son
Just a line hoping you are well as it leaves us fairly well.
Hope the weather has taken up again. It is beautiful today.
I saw Mrs Osborne down town today. She is not very
grand and she said Nora was poorly. Dear Son, your
Uncle Frank was buried yesterday, died on Monday
morning. They never came to say anything. Mary has not
heard from Les this week but the Postman says the mail
went down at Portugal. I heard from Aunt Liz this
morning. She says there is free fights there for food. We
have not seen any tomatoes yet. Ada Walker is over with
the youngest. She don't look very grand. Les Hackett is at
Warrington. They kept him when he went for his medical.
Your Dad has got the rheumatics in his arm. Aunt Liz sent
us a prescription this morning, 16/– a bottle. I don't know
if he will try it.
　　She says 2 houses at Tibshelf were set on fire by
lightning. I have not any more news, my dear, but a letter
seems to cheer you up, so will close, with ever fondest
love to you, I remain your everloving Mam x x x x
Goodnight and God Bless you.

[From George's mother]

Red Brook Lane
19 June

We are having summer weather this week, quite a treat.
We have nearly finished digging for victory in the back
garden. Let's hope it will be soon.

[From Nan]

Swan Inn
28 June

I thought about you last Saturday when I went across the
meadows and saw them all bathing in the river. Remember
when we were first courting and I used to meet you
coming back from bathing?

    My word, we seem to be giving Jerry some stick now
with our big bombs, night and day as well. I'm afraid it
will be a battered Germany when it is over. But I say keep
on pasting him and give them some of what other
countries have suffered.

Swan Inn
21 July

It is rather a pantomine at home at the present time. Dad is
getting quite perturbed about the beer. He has got to tap
his last two barrels of beer tomorrow. The Club has been
closed since yesterday dinner time and, of course, it made
us packed out again. Then there are a lot of strangers
calling in cars and lorries. He won't have enough for his
own customers after Thursday till Saturday night. He is
really worried stiff about it. Anyway, it isn't worrying
me, as you might guess.

Swan Inn
31 July

Mother is busy patching Dad's trousers again. It is all
sewing at our house. It is about half past four as I write this
and if you could just see our kitchen, all upside down, and
we have got to finish upstairs after tea. You would think
we were in a nice mess.

    You see, Dolly is having the gas in today, just when
we could do with her. All the same, she is very pleased
about it, as she has wanted the gas a long time and I believe
it is a nice big cooker she is having.

Swan Inn
2 August

Well, dearest, you will be surprised to know we never
opened at all yesterday, Friday mind you, but we hadn't a
drop left. It came just turned eight this morning, so after
we had tapped the barrels, the customers wanted us to
open at 11 o'clock and, of course, we did. I don't mind,
though. It will be gone all the quicker in the week. I expect
it will be finished up about Wednesday night, so we shall
be able to have a day or two's rest.

Swan Inn
23 August

We sold out last night at half past eight and that means, of
course, we shan't open till Saturday. They have sold out at
the Club too, so you can bet the men's tongues will be
hanging out before the weekend. It was like a swimming
pool the back of the bar on Sunday night, so you can
imagine what it was like. Anyway, we got rid of 6 barrels
from Saturday dinner time to Monday night, so if the
soldiers come back it will be gone as quickly, I suppose.
    My word, I know you will be pleased as it will give
me a nice rest in the week, even if it means extra at the
weekend. It seems very quiet with the bar not being open
at all. Dad seems lost to death all the time.

Swan Inn
16 September

We have got these tank manoeuvres round here today. It is
a game. They are Czechs and you can't tell what they say.
Some of them are in the smoke room. They say they have
got to capture the British and they have done so. It looks
as if we should be in a mess if Jerry invaded, doesn't it?

Swan Inn
30 September

You know, George, I feel so very weary sometimes I have
many a little weep when I am on my own. It's rotten when
you never seem to do anything right for people and when
you don't feel very well yourself. I can't imagine what life
would be like for me if we ever live on our own and I'm
not being shouted at and told what to do.

It seems very quiet without the soldiers who are on
manoeuvres, but we have sold a lot of beer all the same.
They are knocking bitter off us from this week as they are
cutting all the houses down 10 per cent. But this is only the
start, they say. Anyway, we shall definitely be closed
Wed, Thurs, Frid, so, perhaps, I shall feel a bit better when
I have more rest.

Swan Inn
[Mid October]

All the soldiers have gone, except one or two to clear
things up. It is quite official, they will be going abroad and
in the fighting line too, so you can guess where they are
for, poor devils.

Really George, I can honestly say we have never had
such a night since we have been at the Swan. The Sergeant
Major gave a nice speech about how the boys had been
made welcome. And if you really could have seen and
heard how they enjoyed themselves. They did have a
night.

In the finish, they hoisted me Dad shoulder high and
gave him a song. I thought folks would never have
stopped laughing. We have only a few gallons of mild for
tonight, so we are only opening the outdoor.

[From George's mother]

Red Brook Lane
27 October

I heard from Hilda on Saturday. She said Perc was very middling. He had got some boils on his back and she had been ironing him for sciatica. She said it made the tears come.

Red Brook Lane
4 December

I saw Mr Osborne. He said they were killing the pig this morning, so your Dad will be going over to salt it tomorrow night. I am going to make you and Ted a pork pie.
    Mary heard from Les yesterday. He said he should like a feed of fresh vegetables and a pint of beer.

[From Nan]

Swan Inn
7 December

I saw your Mother down the town and she said she was going back to bake the pork pies as she is making one for Ted as well. Well, dear, as you might know, we have had nothing but pig. I am tired of hearing it. Your Dad came last night to salt it, but he says it was a beautiful pig.
    We aren't so busy tonight as nearly all the soldiers have gone home. They are on embarkation leave. It is hard luck, just before Christmas, too, but I expect there will be a lot going abroad now they have started out in Libya.
    There was hot words last night as there was a pint and a half-pint glass broke and one pint glass on Monday night. As you can guess, Dad was nearly mad about it. He says there won't be a b—— glass left at that rate so, of course, they will have to be more careful. And they were all those nice thin glasses too.

Swan Inn
[December]

My word, love, what a call up for the women if the Bill
passes. I think I shall still be spared as it is only single
women and it was strongly pointed out that no soldiers'
wives were needed to go away from home at all. I suppose
they think it might cause strife, as I don't think it would
suit the soldiers putting them in the A T S, and that sort of
life, do you? Especially when they come home on leave
and no wife to see them.

Swan Inn
14 December

Love, as I write this letter to you I feel exhausted. Never have we had such a Saturday night since we have been at the Swan. They are the most unruly lot of soldiers we have ever had. The customers reckoned it wasn't fit for me to have to wait on in the smoke room, so I had to come out after a while.

Jack Houldcroft and Walter Faulkner and Neddy Rowley and the other customers reckoned they felt more than sorry for me. The tears nearly came so in the finish I stopped in the bar. Neddy Rowley called me in the tap room and he said they never ought to be allowed to be so unruly.

I shan't be surprised if they say something to you when you come home. They reckon it isn't decent for me to have to be there and they don't know what you would think if you were here. Especially with me being a married woman. I know they have got to go abroad, but they needn't be like that, need they?

Well, love, I am looking very forward to seeing you next week as you are just the bright bit of sunshine in my life. If it wasn't for you, love, I have no desire to be alive, as my life is nothing to me. I do wish this war was over so you could take me away from this awful low life. It isn't my way of living, you know.

Swan Inn
24 December

Up to now it doesn't look much like Christmas at home here as it is 5 o'clock and no beer yet. I don't expect it will come now, before Xmas so we shall have a nice Xmas to ourselves. It will seem very funny, won't it, being closed?

Swan Inn
27 December

Well, dearest, Christmas 1941 is as good as over. I wonder
if this time next year it will be an Army Xmas again for
you. I *do* hope it isn't and we are settled in a home of our
own, love.

We had the beer come in yesterday afternoon and,
really, last night it was terrible to serve. Not many
soldiers, though. But we couldn't fill beer half quick
enough and we haven't got enough glasses either.

We have been packed out again this dinner time and
they have been singing. As a matter of fact we have only
just turned out, it being 20 minutes to 4 at that. Mother
looks tired out and Dad has an earful of ale, as you might
guess.

We have only beer to sell as the wines and stout and
other bottle stuff is gone in no time.

I believe the soldiers at the Towers had a lovely
Christmas, turkey and pork and plenty of beer, so it
wasn't altogether too bad for them, although, of course, it
would have been nicer for them at home.

Friday afternoon

My dear George,
            Just a small letter to you
hoping that you are alright. This is my third
letter to you this week and I haven't received one
since Monday which was wrote on Saturday, and
I am beginning to wonder whether there is such
a person still as (Mrs Scragg Junior) or are your
letters going elsewhere? I felt quite disappointed
this morning, when there still wasn't one for me
again, so I thought I had better write again.
            Well George love it is a very cold day today
and I am sure ...

... cold on your
... seems to be very
... something perhaps.
...ich have come
... in cases
... on Wednesday
...didn't seem
... just coming
...nobs, picking

...and some ...
...to ...

3

... I do hope please God
...mes round everything
and peace will be
more. Darling I am
...part from each other,
so I am sending
... I am sending
just for you to
...words are so nice
...it to you love
...and a Happy
...too well dear
I thought it
...de of me ...
...gether and ...

To a
Dear One

E. SCRAGG. No. 1659264
367 BTTY. 42nd S/L REGT. R.A.
NO. I TROOP
X c/o GRANGE FARM X
WADDINGTON
LINES.

88

Chapter Six

'BACK IN THE OLD ROUTINE'

George, 1942

Potter Hanworth
[Early January]

I was on guard 11 to ½ past 12 New Year's Eve, so I saw the old one out and the New Year in, love. Did you sit up at home, pidge? I bet you did, for it's nearly always so since I can remember.

We are having some very quiet nights now. I often wonder if he has got anything to come with, for he doesn't seem to have much to me.

We had some visitors this afternoon, love, a Squadron Leader, Flight Lieut and a minister of air craft production. They had come to see how this new system works and they seemed very interested in it.

Potter Hanworth
12 January

We had a night out last night, pidge, just like old times. I had a good dose, on guard 2 to 4 in the afternoon, air co-operation ½ past five to 7, rouser from 8 till 2 in the morning and guard from then to ½ past 3. So I was just about fed up with it all.

A Jerry was brought down in our area. One of our Beaufighters crashed about a mile from us. We hadn't got

any transport, so some fellows from Waddington had to
guard it all night.

Potter Hanworth
16 February

You needn't worry for one moment of my being
unfaithful to you, darling. You are the only one in this
whole world for me, no-one will ever lead me astray. My
love for you will never change, dearest.

    This war seems to go on and on. I often wonder when
it will end. Things don't seem too rosy one way or
another, what with those three ships escaping from Brest.
It makes you wonder if our bombing is having the success
that we are led to believe.

    The weather has been lovely today, just like spring.
But the *sun* will never shine properly until all this strife can
be looked back on like some ugly nightmare.

Potter Hanworth
10 March

We went on a church parade to Waddington yesterday
afternoon as it is warship week round these parts. RAF,
WAAFS, Home Guards and members from the different
ARP services were there, love. It was quite a nice service,
but it was held in the village hall as, you know, the church
was knocked down last summer.

    We were out last night, but nothing came our way,
although a fighter from our nearest station shot down a
Heinkel 111.

    We have our full detachment here now, so things are
much better all round, love.

Potter Hanworth
24 March

I went to Woodhall yesterday, but Ted wasn't there. We
had a decent time and our team won the football cup. The
colonel presented it and said what good games 1 Troop

had played and the officer gave thirty shillings to have it
filled, so we called on the way back and had a drink.

Old Mick sprained his ankle in the last few minutes,
love. I had the job of going to the MOs with him. You'd
have laughed, love, to see us coming back. He was having
a ride on my back.

Potter Hanworth
26 March

I'm looking forward to this time next week when I shall be
with you for seven glorious days, love. I hope the weather
will be as good as it has been these last two days, for it's
been grand, real hot at times.

We went to Waddington for training yesterday. It
warmed us up, bayonet practice and hand grenade
throwing. Mick's ankle has been X-rayed and it's found to
be broken. He's in Bracebridge military hospital, love.
We've had all the beds out today and scrubbed the floor of
the hut. It smells a lot sweeter, but it will be as bad as ever
before long, I suppose, love. We haven't had any
operations of any description for nights. We are having an
easy time of it at present.

Potter Hanworth
9 May

The sarg went on leave this morning, in a temper too. The
guard hadn't woke him up and he had to rush, so I expect
he'll come back the same as he went. If he smiles I'm sure
this war would finish. It's a good job nobody takes any
notice of him, for he'd drive you crackers.

Potter Hanworth
12 May

The sarg came off leave last night, miserable as usual, but
he's gone on a course today, so we've got a few more days
of heaven.

We haven't had any raid on Lincoln yet, but we

expected it last night as forty raiders were reported coming in. But they spread out and the raid fizzled out.

Well, darling, I've made you a ring out of plane glass. I hope it will fit you.

Potter Hanworth
29 May

We've got a night up tonight, 12 till 4 in the morning. I shall just have been up 23 hrs by the time it's over, love. The best of it is, pidge, we've had an hour and a half of it since five o'clock tonight, all in our own time. We are about fed up with it all, it will be heaven when this war is over, darling.

Well, darling, all being well this time next week I shall be with you and, instead of wishing you goodnight, I shall be kissing you goodnight.

Potter Hanworth
[Early July]

The officer complimented us on the gardens last night and said they are the best he's seen. It wouldn't surprise me if he hasn't got his eye on a few things, it's generally the case.

The sarg has taken it into his head to keep rabbits, so Mitch and I have been busy making a couple of hutches for them.

Potter Hanworth
21 July

We've got three rabbits now, but they aren't up to much. The sarg thinks they are great, but he can't tell one from a bull's foot.

Potter Hanworth.
25 July

We had a night out Thursday night, enemy action from
half past 11 to half past one and, to finish off, they had us
on air co-op from 2 till 10 to 4, so we had a belly full. Still,
we had till 12 in bed.

It [the wireless?] said that he had been over the
Midlands, love. I hope he didn't disturb you. Nothing was
dropped near us. The night fighters were in good form, 7
out of forty, love.

Potter Hanworth
[Late July]

We've won Battery, Regimental and entered for
Divisional gardening prizes, so we've done well, haven't
we, pidge? We've been complimented on it by the OC.

Potter Hanworth
4 August

We've had Jerry over practically all this day, so we've
spent a pleasant Aug. Mon. I don't think. I've been
looking at some snaps we had taken when we were at St
Annes. My word, darling, what a contrast then and now.
No clouds to mar our happiness, was there? Still, my
sweetheart, those days will come again and then for some
more glorious times together.

Old Jerry seems to be warming up again, doesn't he?
It's a great pity such things are going on, but I think that
his striking power isn't so great as ours.

He dropped a few bombs on and around Lincoln,
killing one and injuring six. One fell on the nursing home.
All the guns opened up yesterday afternoon. They don't
half make a noise, like bombs themselves, love.

Potter Hanworth
11 August

We've got a day's sports tomorrow at Woodhall. They've got me down for a few events, but I think I've gone past my running days, love. Still, we shall see. There's five pounds to be given out for prize money, so it will make it more interesting.

The rabbits are doing fine. I'll see if I can have three for the next time I come on leave, one each for the children.

Potter Hanworth
14 August

We had a nice afternoon yesterday for the sports. We had a good time, finishing up with a film show, and bless me if it wasn't *Man Hunt*. I didn't mind seeing it again.

I won a couple of prizes, love, one for third place in the 440 yrds and the other in the tug-o-war, beating a team that hadn't lost before. The prizes were a pocket knife and a table knife and fork. I feel stiff today, but we've all been for a run this afternoon, about four miles, so it might take it off.

Potter Hanworth
16 August

The weather is grand today, real summer sunshine, love. It reminds me of the Sunday afternoons we used to go for walks. I wonder how far those days are off now, love. Not too far, I hope.

We had a grand time at the Battery Sports yesterday, love. Our troop carried away the honours for the second year in succession. Number four troop were leading on points before the last event, the final of the tug-o-war, so we'd got to win that to win the day. And we managed it, love. All the team had a pocket knife each as a prize. There was a big crowd there, love, civvies, land army, air force and the whole battery.

Potter Hanworth
19 August

The weather is lovely these past few days and the farmers are busy cutting their corn crops. We are busy wood sawing in readiness for the winter. We've got a grand lot to cut up, having fetched two lorry loads out of Potter Woods. There's no end of hazel nuts in there, love, but they are hardly full yet. I'll do my best to bring you some when I come on leave.

I've got to go to Woodhall for two days on Friday to train in the Battery's tug-o-war team, ready for the Regimental sports on Wednesday. I don't like the idea of it, love.

The champion tug-of-war team, summer 1942; George is number one on the rope.

Potter Hanworth
23 August

We went to Woodhall for our tug-o-war training, but we might as well have stopped here, for there wasn't another team there to pull against, so it was a waste of time.

Potter Hanworth
25 August

A Lancaster crashed about a mile from us, so we all rushed off to it, love. My word, it was a mess. It crashed in some back gardens, just missing the houses, but took all sheds and pigsties with it. Two of the crew were killed and the others escaped. They were very lucky.

We were getting pigs out of the wrecked sties. One was trapped with a burning engine on the roof. We got it off and I tied a rope on it and pulled it to safety. It's a marvel to me that it wasn't killed. The rafters saved it, just leaving enough room for it to sit on its haunches in the corner, love. I don't like going to these crashes, for they are a ghastly sight, but I suppose it's best to give every assistance if you can, love.

Potter Hanworth
27 August

Well, love, it's been the Regimental sports today.

It was raining hard this morning. I thought we were going to have a bad day, but just after dinner the sun broke through and it's been a scorcher.

Our battery won the event with a total of 66 points and 368 were second with 54. Our tug-o-war team won again, love, but, my word, we had to pull this time. Still, we all received ten shillings each, so it was worth it, pidge.

All 367 entries for the sports had their photos taken and the Major took us to the Spa Hotel for a drink out of the Regimental cup. It's been a grand day out, love, and some really good sports to watch.

Potter Hanworth
16 September

I was helping with the harvest yesterday, along with
another fellow. I quite enjoyed it, love. It's a change to get
away from this prison without walls. We put twelve hours
in between us. It should be a good pay bag at the weekend.

I caught a young rabbit in the cornfield and put him in
with the others, but I was looking at it this morning and it
got away. Perhaps it was as well, love, as it was very
frightened.

Potter Hanworth
20 September

I set the snares last night and there was a nice hare in one
this morning. It's in the pot for supper. We had a night
free from rousers of any kind, so we had a good night's
sleep. We haven't been able to fetch any more wood, but
we've got a fair amount by us and it will be very useful this
winter.

*The victorious Searchlights
sports team, summer 1942;
George is in the back row,
fourth from right.*

United Nations Service

Sunday, August 30, 1942, 3 p.m.

To be broadcast from a Cathedral at 7.30 p.m.
(Forces Programme) and throughout the British
Empire and U.S.A., September 6-7

Introductory Service

HYMN—ALL PEOPLE THAT ON EARTH DO DWELL—A.D. 1561

ALL people that on earth do dwell,
    Sing to the LORD with cheerful
        voice ;
Him serve with fear, His praise
    forth tell,
Come ye before Him, and rejoice.

2. For why? the LORD our God is
        good;
    His mercy is for ever sure ;
    His truth at all times firmly stood,
        And shall from age to age
            endure.

3. To Father, Son and Holy Ghost,
    The GOD Whom Heav'n and earth adore,
From men and from the Angel-host,
    Be praise and glory evermore.

PRAYERS

Let us Pray

Let us draw near to God with humility of heart, acknowledging all
that has been amiss in our international relations, beseeching his forgive-
ness and cleansing, and a new consecration to His Service.

(*A brief period of silence*)

We humbly beseech thee, O Father, mercifully to look upon our
infirmities ; and for the glory of thy Name turn from us all those evils
that we most righteously have deserved ; and grant, that in all our
troubles we may put our whole trust and confidence in thy mercy, and
evermore serve thee in holiness and pureness of living, to thy honour
and glory ; through Jesus Christ our Lord. *Amen.*

> *A Prayer for the King and all in Authority in our land*
> *A Prayer for the Allied Nations*
> *The Lord's Prayer (said together)*

LESSON—REV. 21 : 1-5

HYMN—O GOD OUR HELP IN AGES PAST—A.D. 1719

O GOD, our help in ages past,
    Our hope for years to come,
Our shelter from the stormy blast,
    And our eternal home.

3. A thousand ages in Thy sight
    Are like an evening gone ;
Short as the watch that ends
        the night
    Before the rising sun.

2. Beneath the shadow of Thy
        Throne
    Thy Saints have dwelt secure ;
Sufficient is Thine Arm alone,
    And our defence is sure.

4. O GOD, our help in ages past,
    Our hope for years to come,
Be Thou our guard while
        troubles last,
    And our eternal home.

Potter Hanworth
[September]

We pulled up the onions yesterday and got nearly a
hundred pounds in all, so we should last the winter
through, love.

Potter Hanworth
6 October

I think we start sugar beet pulling tomorrow at £3-10-0d
per acre, so we should have some money to share out
when we've done.

Potter Hanworth
20 October

The weather has been rather stormy these last few days
and it makes the beet pulling a bit sticky, although we are
still carrying on with it. The farmer gave us £10 on
account for what we have done, but it will be quite
another week before it's completed, love. If all could work
the same it wouldn't be so bad, but some are very slow.
      We haven't had Jerry for ages and no air co-op for a
few nights now as the weather has been against it. We've
got some big brass hats coming here on Tuesday. This site
has been picked for the job and, I can tell you, it's causing
us some extra work. Of all the sites there is in the
Northern Command, they choose this one.

Potter Hanworth
22 October

Well, love, the big noises have been and everything has
gone off OK. One was Gen Sir Frederick Pile, Chief of
Air Defence of Great Britain. He shook hands with us all
and said the garden and lister were the best in the whole
Command.
      The Colonel has given us the rest of the day off duty.
He said how grateful he was for the work we had done and

would like to give us more time off, but there was a *war* on, love.

The lads are tribing off to Lincoln, but I've got a night off, so I'm waiting in for dinner. I wished I could have got away early this morning and I should have made a flying visit, darling, but I suppose I shall have to wait for my forty-eight hrs, love.

Phil Davis has gone on seven days yesterday. He seemed fed up. I shouldn't be surprised if he failed to return.

Potter Hanworth
29 October

We've finished the one field. He's paid us £24 for what we did and asked us to work in another, but I'll tell you one thing, love, I shan't work like I did, for everyone's had the same pay, 34s each, and some only earned about 4s.

Potter Hanworth
12 November

We told the farmer we didn't think he'd paid us enough for the last field, so he's given us another 50s. He's a decent chap and he says he doesn't want to lose our help just yet.

The news is good, isn't it, love? I can't see it lasting another twelve months. Churchill seems delighted with the progress. Fancy hearing the church bells again, love. [Church bells, which had been silenced throughout the war, reserved for invasion warning, were rung to celebrate the victory of El Alamein.]

Potter Hanworth
19 November

The weather's very cold now, especially in the mornings
as there's no fire kept going during the night.

Phil Davis got seven days C B and six days' pay
stopped. He's got to go to Waddington to do it. The sarg
comes back tomorrow. I hope he's left his miserable ways
behind him.

Potter Hanworth
29 November

I went rabbiting yesterday afternoon, but we had a bit of
bad luck. We only caught two and lost a ferret which cost
the chap 15s. We did a bit of work for the farmer,
emptying patent manure down at the siding. I earned
10s 7d for 8 hrs work.

St Hugh's School
Woodhall Spa
[December]

Well, pidge, the week is passing very nicely. If all courses
were like this one, I wouldn't mind them. No searchlight
work at all, it's a treat to get a break, love.

I was expecting a letter today from you, but perhaps
there wasn't any transport coming into Woodhall from
our troop today.

We haven't really got any need to go out for
entertainment. The padre gave a film show last night,
Gary Cooper in *The Plainsman*. Everybody enjoyed it.
Tomorrow there is one of Bernard Shaw's plays. Perhaps
that won't be so good, though.

Well, love, it will soon be Xmas now, won't it. I can
hardly realise it will be the third one on which we've been
parted, darling. It seems terrible to think about it. I hope
it's the last one. I try to picture next Xmas in a home of
our own and our wish complete. It won't be long before
the little stranger arrives now, will it, dearest? Time will
soon go by after Christmas.

Gnr G Scragg No 1659264
369 Btty 42nd S/L Regt RA.
Potter Hanworth
Nr Lincoln
Lincs.
Tues.

Dear Nan,

Just a line to let you know I'm
alright dear but not so bright as last week
when I knew I was coming to see you love,
however there have gone to-day on their seven
days so perhaps mine will soon work round.
We have had the last three nights very quiet
no planes about at all I hope you have
had it the same love for its very nice to go
to bed in a peaceful sort of mind. Its a
rotten day cold, wet and foggy so we
are having a idle morning for we cant
get on with our cleaning. Well darling I hope
you are quite well and that your cold is
better, take care of yourself sweet. I'm finding
those woolies very useful love these cold days

especically the scarf at night when I am on guard.
I must write and thank Bobby for helmet
and mittens when I have time but its very at
nights now because somebody has swiped our lamp.
I hope Marys eyes are getting better for they
must be very painful to her, but perhaps the
doctor will get more advice if they dont
improve soon. I went to Woodhall H.Q on
Monday for a course of firing and a fellow
told me there was a parcel for Ted there
knocking about for days but it was
good me going for it as they will
nasty send it on to the school love. We
were given ten rounds to fire, five out of the
Enfield five from the Ross but I fired nine
at another chaps target before it was noticed
so I had an more hitting the target only
five times love, but some did worse than that.
Well pidge I will close now for its dinner
time so cheerie duck.
Remember me From your everloving sweetheart
to them all love.   George xxxxxxxxxxxx XX

Chapter Seven

'ALWAYS CHASING RAINBOWS'

Nan, 1942

Swan Inn
12 January

We had Jerry on Saturday night. The windows rattled a
bit, but they fetched one of them down between
Tamworth and Nuneaton. Frank was on the post at the
time and saw the plane come down. One managed to bale
out, but the others were all killed.

[From George's mother]

Red Brook Lane
4 February

Your dad has got the screws in his hip. We got the bacon
out of salt last night. Mary has heard from Les. He says his
arm is in a sling with an abscess under it and he will go to a
rest camp when he is a bit better. I have got you a record of
'Yours' and 2 flints.

[From Nan]

Swan Inn
22 February

I am so sorry to tell you that Timmy Binfield got killed on
Friday afternoon. Somehow or other he got in between a
trailer and it dragged him right from Charlie Carthy's
butcher's shop down to the siding gates. It cut one of his
legs right off and some of his body parts were flung all
over the place. His insides came right out. I believe he was
cut up to bits, one of the worst accidents ever known
round here. You know Bill, the soldier who lodged at
Gordon's? Well, his wife saw it and she went to him and
he just spoke to her before he died. Poor lad, it is a shame,
isn't it?

Swan Inn
4 March

David is rather poorly with irritation between his little
legs. He can't sleep at night. The Nurse says after all Mary
will have to have him circumcised. She told Mary she once
knew a young man that got married when he was 27 and
he had to have his done before he could get married. She
said he didn't half bless his mother for not having it done
when he was a baby. Mary is going to have it done straight
away now she knows, as she says she wouldn't like it to
prevent him having children when he grows up.

Swan Inn
19 March

I have got a bit of sad news for you, George. You know
that young soldier who was at Gordon's? His wife is still
there and the poor girl had news yesterday morning from
the War Office that Bill was one of the missing in Malaya.
I saw her today, poor girl, and she looked so upset. It isn't
much for her to live for, with two little children to rear on
her own.

[To Nan from N Wright (a friend)]

21 Langley Avenue
Somercotes
Derby
30 March

Thank you for your kindness in sending me the wool. I am
pleased to say it did the trick and I have been able to finish
my jumper. When I was unable to get any more wool I
began to think it meant pulling it undone.

As yet we don't appear to be making much progress,
but we must keep our chins up and have faith. I often
picture to myself the transformation when we shall be able
to have the lights blazing and see the streets and buses all
lighted up again. What a thrill it will be. I don't go far in
the blackout.

Olive's soldier boy has joined the Commandos.

[From George's mother]

Red Brook Lane
3 May

I expect you have heard of the Italian prisoners getting
loose. They have caught 7 out of the ten. The Home
Guard were out all Monday and at night one Home Guard
got shot in the knee. He is in Walsall Hospital.

[From Nan]

Swan Inn
7 May

A soldier has just been in for some cigs and he has told us
they are all going tomorrow and there won't be any more
soldiers coming at all, as the Towers has been fixed for a
drilling place for the Home Guard. I suppose it will be for
the duration of the war, so it looks as if we have done with
the soldiers.

Swan Inn
31 May

My word, love, by wireless at dinner time, it seems as
though we shall soon be making the Germans squeal. It
sounded lovely when they gave it out that over a thousand
bombers went over. I do hope the people will cry out
against it as I am sure we will soon let them know what air
warfare means. I hope that he won't return those thousand
bombers on us, but, somehow, I don't think he's got so
many to come with now.

At Dolly's
22 June

Another big setback for us in Libya with them taking
Tobruk again. It seems we aren't strong enough to hold
him anywhere, doesn't it? It makes us wonder how many
years it's going to last. I get awful fed up sometimes and I
expect you do too, love. It's just an existence, that's all.
    What did you think of the fight on Saturday? I was
rather disappointed as I should like to have seen the older
man win. However, I think Freddie Mills well deserved
the win, as he must have given him a jolly good pounding
to have knocked him out of the ring like that.

Swan Inn
18 July

Mary and Ted and his Dad went to the Hippodrome. She
said it was lovely. There was a man singing, imagining a
soldier was taking his little boy on his knee. It was for
young couples who love children. Mary said it brought
tears to your eyes, but it was a lovely show.

Swan Inn
[Late July]

I believe the bombing was bad at Wolverhampton and
Walsall. Alice and Hazel came yesterday and said when her
Dad went to work it was bombed out. It's made rather a
mess of Birmingham. Smiths, where we used to go, is
down to the ground and they had got a lot of furniture
stored for people. It's knocked no end of big shops down
and they said the road was running with blood.

Swan Inn
[Late August]

It was very sad about the Duke of Kent, wasn't it? In fact,
about all of the crew.

Swan Inn
[Autumn]

As it seems so quiet and strange without you, I decided to
go to the concert after all and I'm jolly glad I did too. It
was excellent, George. I never went to such a good concert
before. The acrobating alone was outstanding. Talk about
the circus at Blackpool. It couldn't touch this fellow and he
was only an ordinary private. I am sure he must have been
in that sort of thing before he joined up. And there was a
violinist, he was marvellous. Really, it was extra good, the
whole show. Talk about talent. Everybody said they were
too good to be in the Army, but there you are, even the
clever ones aren't counted any different with this war.

*A birthday card from Nan to
George.*

Swan Inn
25 October

Mother hasn't been very grand since last Wednesday. I'm
sure she looks very poorly, George. My Dad isn't a bit fair
to her, you know, as she's worth a far better life than she's
having to lead at this place. He'll never know the worth of
her till she's gone, love.

As you know, it never was a bed of roses at the best of times, but it makes me feel very uncomfortable as, of course, I can't do the same as I used to do as I've got the little stranger to think of as well as myself.

Swan Inn
29 October

I am just longing for that day when we shall all be happy and united together. It will be so nice, except for those whose loved ones will never come back. It seems so awful wicked.

Swan Inn
21 November

It's beginning to look very dismal now in the afternoons, especially with all the blackouts and nothing much to buy. I know there are many hearts that will always ache for their loved ones and can never be happy again.

There are quite a few of the boys on leave this week.

They haven't half had a sing song in the bar this dinner time, I can tell you. They might as well, though, as you never know where the poor lads are going to be sent, do you?

Swan Inn
[Late November]

Well, love, the war news seems very much better now, doesn't it? Things seem to be going in our favour now. I wonder what Mr Churchill will have to say tonight.

There's one thing, he can begin to gloat over our gains now. What about the French fleet scuttling itself before letting the Germans have it? It shows which side they are on, but it's a pity they didn't let us have it in the first place.

These are nasty, dark days just before Christmas, aren't they? I hate it when it's like this and you have to blackout so soon.

Mother is just going to have the European news on. She does like the wireless on, I can tell you. They have wrote and told Dad he can have what beer he likes as there is plenty now, so it looks as if things must be improving somewhat. It will be like old times, won't it? He is very pleased about it.

Swan Inn
12 December

Christmas will soon be here and there is nothing for anyone to look forward to, is there? When we went to Stafford on Tuesday there wasn't anything for the little children. We looked all over the place today for something for the Xmas tree, but we couldn't get a thing.

Swan Inn
[Mid December]

Well, love, you will be surprised to know that poor old Lil has been done the dirty on. One of the sergeants from up at Flaxley Green has been good enough to let Lily know that that chap she is going with is a married man with two children, and they are cripples at that. Isn't he a dirty rotter, kid? I believe she is very cut up about it and was in tears at work the other day. Of course, he has cleared out now as he has been removed from Flaxley somewhere else.

The money she has spent on him. Only last week she bought him a lovely wallet for 9/6. I do think it's a let down for the poor girl. I hope, she learns a lesson from it. It shows you never know anybody, do you?

I know you wouldn't do anything wrong, but it worries me with those other chaps there, if they try to lead you off. I should hate anything like that, as I am so bitter against those sort of carryings on.

Baby Dorothy.

Chapter Eight

'BABY MINE'
1941–1943

1941

[From Nan]

Swan Inn
[Early 1941]

Dear, I am writing to ask you what I should do, as they are talking in the papers of conscripting the women. I feel worried stiff about it, as the registration begins early next month. You see, love, I really have no excuse, as I don't think I should stand much chance of getting out of it, should I?

I don't think I should like the idea of going to Birmingham, especially working at nights, because of the bombing, so I wondered whether I should get a job on the bank.

I feel terribly worried about it. Fancy, they have got you there, and now they want me there as well. Perhaps you will tell me what to do, love. If it does become compulsory, I reckon I shall have to go. I can't work in comfort today for thinking about it.

Mother and Mary are worried to death about me going to munitions, especially our Mary. I ought to be having a baby and then the problem would be solved right away. I shall be so pleased to see you again a week on Friday, George, and then, perhaps, you can talk to me about it.

Same address.

My dearest Nan,
                Well darling I've
arrived back safe after the worst
journey I've ever had. I didn't
get into camp till five to eleven
and was on guard till a part
12 so I am sending the cards and
just writing a short note as it
is nearly 1 o-clock and we are on
concentrations in the morning. love.
Well darling don't worry like
you are doing for I'm sure it
isnt good for you and it wont
help matters any. If you would
rather let it drop for the time
being you can do but you seemed
so ansciou to find out what was
the reason so now if you feel
like waiting until the circumstances
are more favourable I shan't

mind in the least, but we must have our happiness some time love. I'll leave it entirely to your own judgement weither you carry on with it or not darling, for I know how worried you are about it all. Well dearest I will write again as I feel about ready to fall asleep as I stand here so hoping you will find some little pleasure out of Christmas I will close now,

From your everloving husband

George X X X X X

X X X X X X X X

I shall always love you darling come what may you are the only one for me.

Swan Inn
[April]

I am feeling a bit better, but it has put the tin hat on it, as I have definitely got to register. I bet I shall have to go. There is only one thing that will stop me, and you have said you won't do the necessary as it would worry you too much. So I suppose I must be brave and go with the others. I know which I would sooner do, though.

Well, dear, Bevin means to have out of us all he can, but I don't expect it will hit these toffs much. [Ernest Bevin was Labour Minister in the wartime Government.] They will find some excuse, I expect. It will be working class again who will have to do their stuff.

Fancy Bevin calling women up! I shall tell them I have got you there, they don't want me as well. In fact, I don't know what to register for.

Swan Inn
12 May

My word, there are some babies coming along. Hannah Conway's having another, and Ruby Samuels, who married Harold Harvey, is having one. All but me. I think I shall have to get a new husband and see what can be done, don't you?

Someone asked your mother if we'd got any family and she told them we were going to wait till the war was over, so I think we shall have to wait, if you think it's the best. But all the same I feel a wee bit envious about it, you know.

Swan Inn
[May]

Mary is just sorting out her baby clothes upstairs, which I *do* hope will be needed this time. They are all beautiful, George. I expect her mind went back a bit while she was looking over them. I have just finished that little outdoor suit for her. It does look nice.

How I wish I was going to look forward to one of my

own, but perhaps I am going to be one of those unlucky ones in life, deprived of that which is most cherished in my estimation. Never mind, I suppose I mustn't get downhearted, must I?

Swan Inn
[May]

We are busy spring cleaning. I told you we were going to make a start. We are going to get it all nice and clean ready for September, and by then I hope I shall be looking forward to ours. I shall be so *very* happy about it George, as I love you so much. That's why I want one so much. Try and stick to your promise, darling, and I will look after myself.

[From George]

Waddington
Lincolnshire
31 May

Well, love, we have come back to the old spot, as you can see by the address, so there is no need to worry about me going abroad as yet.

I was pleased to know you had started to be unwell for, as I told you, love, I want to mean it when we do. It won't be long now, will it, my precious?

[From Nan]

Swan Inn
3 June

I shall be so pleased to see you, love, as it seems an awful long time since you came home. I am looking forward to that promise, George. I shall be more satisfied then, love. It's no use waiting till the war is over, as I think we shall wait a long time, love. Never mind. Wait till you come home, love, we will give them a surprise.

[From George]

Waddington
16 June

Three went altogether on seven days leave, so I hope I can manage to stop here for another five weeks so that I can have mine, pidge.

We shall know by then if our wish is coming true, won't we, darling? I hope it does and you go on alright, precious. Won't it be a surprise for them, darling, when they know? I know somebody who will make a fuss of it, and if it doesn't suit some of the others, it's our responsibility, isn't it, love?

I'm pleased you are looking forward to it in the right way, for I'm sure everything will be for the best.

Waddington
17 June

Darling, I'm anxiously waiting to know the result of our secret, aren't you, my precious? I hope it's not been in vain.

[From Nan]

Swan Inn
24 June

I felt a lot better than I did, and not so downhearted since I wrote to you on Saturday. I have been looking through that book we had when we were married and I now know why it didn't act. When you are both in good health it is quite natural to give way to your feelings and nothing need happen.

As it was, however, it was just a fortnight after I had been unwell, and of course, as it says in the book, if you are both healthy it only takes effect seven days before my period and three days after.

Well, dear, I should very much like you to be able to have your seven days leave either the 11th or the 18th, but the 18th would be preferable, as on that day I should be unwell, and then before you went back it would be just the exact time, as it says in the book it is three days after which should be the best bet. If you come home on the 11th, it will be just before I should, so it won't matter, we can just the same. Look what you've missed all this long time and the thrills you could have had! Never mind, you will know another time.

I'll bet you will think me a right one looking all this up, won't you? Never mind, though. I hope it will be worth knowing. I *do* hope you won't have to have your leave changed again, as I doubt it would act unless I was just so.

Well, dear, take care of yourself, as you know how much I love you. That's why I want my baby to be just like you, when we shall be lucky enough to have one.

[From George]

Waddington
25 June

Just a few lines, love, hoping you are alright and not worrying too much over our disappointment. Don't think that it is your fault, darling. It may be mine, or perhaps neither, for nature plays some curious tricks at times, love.

We must try again when I have my seven days, for if we are strong and healthy, it doesn't mean that it is bound to take effect the first time, darling.

You know, sweetheart, I think we were a bit too confident. Still don't get downhearted, as I think neither of us are lacking in our parts. So better luck next time, dearest.

Waddington
29 June

Darling, according to your letter this morning, Ted and I will be on our seven days together. But I'm sorry, love, I can't arrange mine for the 11th or 18th. I shall have to be satisfied with it, although, as you say, it would be more convenient on either of those dates to try again, love.

Well, my precious, the topmost thought on my mind today has been you, love, and how you went on registering. I sincerely hope you don't have to go away, dear. Somehow, I don't think you will, but let me know the result of it, won't you?

Waddington
12 July

My precious, it's been a lovely week. I've enjoyed every minute of it, darling, and I hope you have. But don't get down, love. It won't be long before I see you again.

Do let me know if anything becomes of our efforts, love. I hope it won't be the same as the last time, still, we must keep on trying.

[From Nan]

Swan Inn
16 July

I am so sorry to have to write and tell you of our big disappointment again. As I told you in my last letter, I thought it would be of no avail. I started to be unwell on Wednesday night, quite a bit before I should have been. It shouldn't have been until today.

Dear, I told you when you were at home that I didn't have any pain, well, I can tell you, I have made up for it this time. Oh, George, I can't tell you how I feel about it. I feel as though it's my fault and I have failed you.

But, I tell you this, if it doesn't turn successful the next time I shall see what can be done about it and consult Dr Abbot. It might mean a slight operation, you know, but at all costs I shan't rest till I am able to have that precious son.

You see, when you come home in August, it will be just a little too soon again, I think, but I bet you will have a *very* good try this next time.

[From George]

Waddington
23 July

Just a few lines hoping you are alright, darling, and not too
cut up over our disappointment, for I'm sure it can't
always fail to take effect, love. We must go on trying until
we get our desire. It's worth trying hard for, isn't it? I'm
sure neither of us will be satisfied until we have succeeded.

[From Nan]

Swan Inn
16 September

I haven't got the heart to interest myself in anything. I feel
as though I shall go mad if it doesn't happen soon. It's
really beginning to get me down, so when you come
home you will really have to do your *very* best. Somehow,
I think we shall manage it next time.

[From George]

Waddington
17 September

Well, darling, I received your letter this morning, love,
but I don't like to hear of you being so depressed. You
mustn't let it get to you to such an extent as that, love, for
I'm sure we shall eventually get our desire, so please don't
let it worry you so much, darling. You ought to go to the
whist drives, love. It would be a little change for you and
break the monotony of staying in every night.

[From Nan]

Swan Inn
18 September

Well, dear, I went with Dolly after all last night, as I felt so depressed and disappointed I thought a little change would take it off a bit. It was a big success, there being thirty-seven tables for the whist, and it was simply packed for the dancing, but it was only on till twelve.

I had one or two dances with the soldiers I know that come in the bar, but I don't get very familiar with them as I don't feel very interested in anybody or anything with worrying so much over our disappointment.

Swan Inn
23 September

Well, dearest, first of all I must tell you that the happy event we have been waiting for has arrived. Mary has got a handsome little son, the exact image of Ted, and I am so pleased to tell you everything was a natural birth.

He is a real beauty and he isn't marked anywhere. They had fetched the Doctor, but he had just been born when he arrived. Well, George, he has got the sweetest face and lovely blue eyes like Ted.

It did seem a shame his father wasn't there to share their happiness, for I am sure Mary is as proud a Mother, as ever could be. It was such a nice birth at the end, he didn't have to be mauled around like the other poor little chap was. He is just like him, George.

Well, darling, now for my bit of news. I was talking to Doris on Saturday. Bob has just been on seven days. Really, George, when I tell you, you will be surprised. I don't know how it was, but she started telling me about her Aunty being married 11 years and she has just had a little son last week. She has always wanted one, but has had to wait a long time, hasn't she?

Well, George, Doris and Bob are in the same predicament as we are. She opened her heart to me and told me how terribly disappointed she and Bob are, and the worst of it is, Bob blames Doris. They have been

trying ever since Bob went in the Army, and you know
how long that is, kid.

When you come home I have got such a lot to tell you
about it, George, but Doris told me on Saturday that they
think they have had their wish fulfilled, as she has gone a
week over her time. She can remember the particular night
and told me everything about it. She is coming home in a
fortnight's time, and she is coming to tell me. I do hope
she has her wish, as she says Bob is so very keen on a baby.

Oh, George, another thing, dearest. On all accounts
stick to the date of your leave, darling, as I have thought it
all out and it will be just right. I shall just about be on and
then it will be just right after.

So, please, love, don't have it altered, will you, as
when you see our Mary's little one, I am sure you will
want one of our own.

Swan Inn
25 September

Well, dear, if you could just see our house, you wouldn't
half smile. Ted came an hour ago, and if you could have
seen his face when he saw his fine, big son, you would
have been pleased.

It is a handsome baby, George, weighing 7¾ lbs
dressed. I have just had him in the fresh air for half an hour
along the road.

I felt so proud of him, but how much prouder if he
had really been my very own! Oh, George, I seem to
handle him so well and, really, I'm not jealous of Mary
and Ted, but I should like one of my own to love.

But if nothing happens when you come home, I shall
go and see Doctor Abbot. Since you have gone back, I
think I know why it hasn't happened. I couldn't explain in
a letter, but, as I have told you, don't have the leave altered
if you can help it.

I am very anxious for you to have your leave, as,
really, I don't know what I shall do if we can't have one of
our very own. Everyone tells me I ought to follow in
Mary's footsteps, but they don't know why I haven't, do
they, love? I have wondered many a time about Doris, you
know. I do hope she had her wish.

[From George]

Waddington
26 September

Well, darling, I'm very pleased to know that Mary's happy event has taken place and that both are well. I bet you are all pleased that it's a boy. I told you I thought it would be.

I hope that we are able to achieve our desire during my seven days, love. If not, I think it would be best to see the doctor. I bet you and Doris had a real conflab over the subject, didn't you, love?

But it shows you, darling, there are many more, apart from us, who are a bit mystified as to why they can't have their wish.

[From Nan]

Swan Inn
28 September

I shall be so pleased when you come home, as I love you so much, dear. I feel ever so nice towards you lately, so perhaps I shall feel a bit more thrilled, you know what I mean, when you come home.

It will be no use unless we both feel the same way. And, by jove, if you don't give a good response, there will be ructions about it!

[From George]

Waddington
[October]

Well, dearest, I think we have really done our very best to obtain our desire this time. If nothing comes of it, I shan't know what to think. However, I do hope that it will succeed.

Mary has got a lovely little son, hasn't she, love? I do hope he goes on alright, but, darling, I shall not rest until we have one, no matter how long it takes.

Don't worry too much, and be careful for the time being, until we know for sure whether or not our attempts are successful. I shall be thinking of you, my treasure, during the next month or so more than ever. I hope that when the time comes you will be able to break the glad news to

Your everloving husband
George x x x x x x x

[From Nan]

Swan Inn
8 November

Now, dearest, I am hardly able to tell you how disappointed we both will be, as I started to be unwell on Tuesday night, and, by jove, I know it, too. The pains I have been through have been awful. I have hardly been able to walk about, but imagine how I feel about it. I think we shall have to have a divorce and you get a fresh woman.

[From George]

Potter Hanworth
10 November

Don't talk about getting a divorce, love, for you know whatever our disappointments are in life, you have always got me to share them, as you are all in all to me. So please don't write in that strain, darling. It wasn't a very encouraging letter, was it, love? For I don't like to think of you being so unhappy at home.

[From Nan]

Swan Inn
[Mid November]

Dearest, I have seen the doctor. He came to see the baby yesterday and I explained to him as best I could. However, he said I wasn't the first one by any means, as he has had fifty cases like mine.

But I warn you, dearest, that I have a lot of processes to go through, and *even then* might still be disappointed. He was quite frank about it and told me only twelve out of the fifty were successful.

The first thing he has got to do is examine me, but he wants to have a talk with you first, so he wants you to ring him up when you are on your 48 hours leave and he will come over to see us.

He explained exactly what he thought it was. I have got to have injections. He wants to see you because I expect it will mean an operation and then the injections again for about three months. He asked me if I had ever been pregnant and, of course, I told him no.

Anyway, it seems I have a lot to go through before I can ever have one, but I would go through all that if we could have our desire.

Oh, George, I don't know whatever I shall do if he says it's hopeless. A friend of his, he told me, was just the same and he had his wife in a big hospital at London that cost them £200 and had her split right open, an awful ordeal to go through. And when she came home, they told her before she came away it was a hopeless case. He says they are terribly upset about it.

Anyway, I will try to look on the bright side of things. Your Mary came over yesterday. In fact, she was here while the doctor was here and, after he had gone, I told her and our Doll.

They said they don't think you will ever give your consent for me to go through all that, but it's our affair, isn't it, love?

I shall be glad to see you, though, as you know I shall fret ever so if it is my fault, because I know you would like a baby as much as I should. I don't mind what I go through, dearest, as I know I have got to if I want one.

Well, I don't know what you will think about my letter, but don't worry too much, as I shan't do anything till you come home. And if you want me to leave it till the war is over and you are at home, I will do so, as I know you will be very anxious about me, especially if it means an operation.

But, love, as for myself, I am quite willing to go through with it all, but I do hope it won't be for nothing.

[From George]

Potter Hanworth
15 November

Darling, I am pleased you have mentioned our problem to the doctor. I've been trying to think out the best plan for us, love and I've come to this conclusion. It would be best for us to wait until after the war, but, in the meantime, keep trying, darling, as really the doctor doesn't know for certain what the trouble is, does he?

I wouldn't like you to go through all that ordeal unless I was close by you, darling. It would just about worry me to death. It would, no doubt, be a success, but a lot would depend on the circumstances you were living under, so I think if we waited until we are settled in a home of our own, the better chance of success. Don't you think so, darling?

I should very much like to have a talk with the doctor and perhaps I should get a different view of it all. But I don't think I'd consent for an operation, darling, if it put you in the least danger, as I would never forgive myself.

You know, dearest, whether we are disappointed or not, you mean everything to me and if God wishes us to have our desire, we shall, chance what any doctor can do.

Well, darling, I hope you can see my point of view, but we shall have to talk it over more intimately when I come on leave. So, until then, love, keep your spirits up and hope for the best.

[From Nan]

Swan Inn
24 December

First of all, dearest, I must thank you for the most beautiful Christmas card you have sent me. That is worth far more to me than an expensive present.

Please don't think me unkind for not sending you one, but I haven't sent a Christmas card to anyone, as I feel so very worried about the little problem of ours. But I have made my mind up what to do.

After a lot of thinking, and I have had a talk with mother about it, I have decided to please you, dearest. As mother says, after the war is over, perhaps I shall always regret not having it done.

That is really what you get married for, isn't it? And what could be nicer than this time next year to have a little son or daughter of our own?

I am sure that is what you would really like me to do, isn't it? And I don't mind what I go through, as long as you promise me I shan't have a family in no time. When Dr Abbot comes I shall tell him I shall go to

Wolverhampton. *Please* don't think me unkind for not
sending you a nice card, but this has been topmost on my
mind all the time since Sunday.

Well, love, make the best of your Christmas. I know
we can't feel very happy under the circumstances, being
separated from each other, as when you love each other so
much, it seems awfully hard.

[From George]

Potter Hanworth
26 December

Well, my dearest, I'm pleased you've made up your mind
over what to do on solving our problem, love, and I hope
neither of us will regret going through with it.

If it had been a serious job, love, I wouldn't have
consented to have it done, but the doctor said there was no
danger whatsoever. So I hope when it is done we shall be
able to have our wish that has been evading us for so long.

Don't worry about us having a big family, love. I'll
see that you have no more than you want.

[From George's mother]

Red Brook Lane
[Undated]

Mary has heard from Les this morning. He says he has
heard from you and hopes you are well. Les says put you
and Nan in a bag and see which is addled. You cannot be
after passing the Army doctor. Still, I hope you will have
luck in the future.

1942

[From George]

Potter Hanworth
8 February

My dearest Nan
Well, darling, I hope you are feeling alright on this, our third wedding anniversary, love.

My word, pidge, who would have thought that all this strife would have parted us so soon? We haven't had much married life up to now, darling, but we shall have to make up for lost time when peace is restored once more.

I've thought of that day on a good many occasions today. Lots of things have gone through my mind, love. We have had it pretty rough, but I love, you, as no-one can love more. I've never regretted it, darling, and we've had our share of disappointments, haven't we?

I think our world of roses will come someday, love, and those are the ones I'm living for.

Goodnight my dearest, and may God bless you always. I've looked at our wedding photo many times today, love.

From your everloving husband, George.

[From Nan]

Swan Inn
[Early March]

Dr Abbot called on Friday afternoon, and when he opened the letter it said the operation might be necessary if there was no other way.

But I think somehow, love, it's entirely up to ourselves to try as hard as we can. That specialist distinctly told me seven months wasn't very long to try for a baby, as when we have been actually evading it, he said, such a lot of birth control takes some time before it takes action.

You see, love, it has got to properly catch to make a job of it, as I am so small.

Anyway, I know how it *should* be when the intercourse takes place, so when you come home, it will be me that will have the say this time. I really think we shall manage it. I shall soon know, as I should start to be unwell on the Monday after you have gone back. I *do* hope we are successful, this time, love.

Swan Inn
[Early March]

Dearest, I am really very anxious for you to come home. Dr Abbot came to see Fanny's little boy next door yesterday, so I told her to tell him to call.

Love, I asked him about me having the operation done in a private nursing home, and he says he will make arrangements for that, but he says that it is *most* essential that you should be examined to make perfectly sure that you are alright. You see, love, he told me that he wants everything possible done as the last thing he wants is the operation. But he says that he fears it will have to be done. I can quite understand what he means, love, as you know operations are always serious.

He says he's no doubt you are OK, but he will not allow me to go away till he is sure. Well, dearest, I am writing to ask you, as he is making arrangements for it. You see, I have got to phone him a week before you come home.

Well, love, I should very much like to talk it over with you, but as we can't, I am just going to ask you one thing. When we were married, we said we loved each other and were willing to do anything for each other. Well, love, this is the time you are being put to the test to prove your love for me. Remember Dr Abbot telling me what a lot I have got to go through before I can have my baby? I am quite willing to do everything in my power to have my wish fulfilled, and so I am asking you if your love is great enough just to do that to please me. After all, it is me that has to suffer.

[From George]

Potter Hanworth
4 March

You know, love, that my love for you is one that I would do anything for you. Having to have that exam is no real test of my love. I'm prepared to go through anything for you, darling, and if that's all that stands in the way of our desire being carried on, well, love, you need not worry one scrap over my not having it done.

You needn't worry one moment over my decision, as I am longing for our little son just as much as you are. So goodnight, my dearest, and may God bless us and crown all our troubles with success.

From your everloving husband.
x x x George x x x

PS I had such a peculiar dream last night, darling. I dreamt of our wedding all over again, love. Everything was exactly the same as on that happy day.

[From Nan]

Swan Inn
19 March

I have been a nice walk with Mary and David this afternoon. All the young mothers were out with their babies with it being so fine, and it really makes me so unhappy when I see them all. It makes me feel so lonely somehow. Perhaps this time next year I shall have my wish fulfilled.

Swan Inn
[Early April]

Darling, I expect you will be surprised to hear from me so soon, but you will be very pleased when you know why.

I won't keep you guessing any longer, as I am sure you will want to know. When Mary and I were coming up from the station yesterday we ran straight into Dr Abbot and, of course, he stopped his car. He said the report had come through from Stafford and you are absolutely OK.

He says the results were splendid, so, of course, love, you have gained something with going and now your part is over. He told me the fault lay with me and, you will be surprised when I tell you, I shall be going in the Nursing Home this coming Monday.

He wants it all over before my next period, which, as you know, is due a week on Monday. He is fixing everything up and he was going to get in touch with Dr Maslem Jones today to make the necessary arrangements.

Anyway, it sounds as if it's Wolverhampton I shall be going to, as it's that doctor that will do it. I am feeling a bit nervous, love, and I shan't be sorry when it's all over. Oh, love *please* don't worry about me, as I shall be alright. Then, when you come home, with God's blessing, we shall be able to have our dearest wish fulfilled.

[From George]

Potter Hanworth
11 April

Well, darling, your letter came as a surprise, and a very pleasant one, too. I didn't think the result would be known to us yet, but it's come as a relief to me. I thought it would be OK, but, of course, there's always the outside chance of it not being so, love.

Darling, I'm pleased that he is arranging things so that it will soon be over. I don't like it hanging on now. The suspense isn't very good for us, love.

I wish I were at home, love, so that I could go and see you, but, still, my thoughts will be with you until I hear from you again, darling. You will be always in my prayers and I hope that the ordeal won't be too much for you and that you won't suffer. I wish I were to go through it for you, darling.

[From Nan]

The Nursing Home
Wolverhampton
18 April

Love, first of all I must thank you for ringing up to see how I was getting on. As the Nurse told you, I am going on very nicely.

I know you will be very anxious to get a letter from me and to know how things went on. I must tell you that the Dr was very pleased with the operation and he said it was a very straightforward case.

All the tubes leading from the womb have been tested and stretched. He said there is no reason at all why I shouldn't have my baby, as, of course, all below there has been stretched. He says everything should be easy enough now.

However, I haven't got to wear a ring, as it doesn't need one, but I have got to take special tablets from Dr Abbot. He has written to him about it, and I have got to take them every fortnight, as he wants to make doubly sure those tubes don't get filled up again.

I told the nurse you would be coming home soon and she said I ought to have good results right away. It was with being so small, all the organs of my body had been stretched. Anyway, love, I am feeling much better, but I was feeling very poorly on Thursday when I came out of the anaesthetic, as I was in that for 3½ hours. My tummy just feels as though it's been pinched to pieces and it's very awkward if I am in one position too long. I am going to get up a little bit tomorrow as I am going home on Monday.

Mary and mother came to see me yesterday and Dr Maslem Jones happened to come in to see me while they were here. He asked if that one was my twin, and she told him that she had had two babies. He turned to me and said that I should soon be catching her up. He told mother there was nothing to worry about as everything was just as it should be.

I am anxiously waiting now for you to come home, as it will be nice to be able to talk to you about it. I can't put it all in a letter. I do hope we shan't be disappointed, but I

The bills for Nan's gynaecological operation.

don't think we shall, as the Dr wouldn't tell me if he didn't feel so sure. I have had every attention, love, and am in a most lovely room.

I nearly forgot to tell you the cost of it all, but I don't mind that now I feel I have done my duty. The operation was £10.10s, the anaesthetic £2.2s, and the days I have been in the Home about £5.5s, so that all together it won't be much under £20. But I quite expected that, as, you see, love, I have had everything of the best. You know, love, he is the second to best, finest womb specialist in England, so I feel you will feel satisfied with everything.

I expect your thoughts will often be with me this weekend, and I shall be glad when Monday comes myself, as I am in a room on my own, and the day seems to drag sometimes.

Swan Inn
25 April

Dr Abbot called in to see me yesterday and I had a nice little chat with him. I asked him if I should ever had had my baby if I hadn't had the operation and he said definitely no. But he said that there was nothing to stop it as I am perfectly in order. He did smile, George, when he left me, as he said, 'Well, you know what to do now, it's up to you,' as Dr Maslem Jones said it ought to act straightaway in his letter to Dr Abbot.

I do hope it does, then it will just be round our Wedding Day, won't it, love? It would be lovely, but I suppose I mustn't have too high hopes of it, although they wouldn't tell me that if there was no hope.

I'm looking very forward to seeing you on Wednesday, so I hope you are up to scratch so you can do your best for me.

Swan Inn
[Mid July]

Love, I have just been having five minutes on the sofa, as I get so very tired somehow these days. I get the indigestion awful first thing in a morning. Well, some mornings I have it till I'm sick with it.

I don't know whether it IS this important stranger that's doing the mischief or not, but I think I have gone too far now, love.

However, as I've told you, I'm not getting too thrilled about it, as, until I've seen the doctor, I'm not going to believe it. It seems too good to be true.

Swan Inn
[Mid July]

I feel sure that God has answered our prayers. I never felt so sure of anything before. I am really very thrilled about it, and I'm sure you will be, love, won't you? My back is so bad, though. I do hope everything will be OK. It has really been worth trying for, hasn't it? You see what perseverance does?

If it is that, and I feel sure it is, as I feel different somehow, and I haven't come on again, it won't be very much like me, as you had all the say, didn't you?

I really can hardly believe it, though. I do think God has been so very kind to us, don't you? I bet you will start being worried stiff about me, but you needn't, love, as our baby comes first.

How lovely it will be to look forward to our dear little stranger, won't it?

May God Bless you, and keep you safe always. I'm so longing to see you again

From your everloving wife, Nan.

xxxxxx

Swan Inn
21 July

The Dr called yesterday. Of course, he wanted to know quite a few things. He says there's every reason to think that I should be like that. He'd sooner say there was something than not. However, he's coming to see me in another month's time, so I expect it means an exam again.

He *was* surprised, George, and thought it was jolly good work. Of course, he can't say for sure till he's seen me again, so I'm not thinking too much about it. But he made me smile when he said he was sure we could say the flags were flying!

[From George]

Potter Hanworth
25 July

Darling, I was very pleased to hear from you and to know that our hopes are still high. I don't think that you will come on now. I hope not, for we should both be very disappointed if it didn't succeed.

I'm sorry that you are feeling so poorly, darling, but take care what you eat and get something to ease your indigestion.

[From Nan]

Swan Inn
[Early September]

The Doctor came yesterday and examined me. Well, love, he didn't hesitate to tell me that our great desire is going to be fulfilled.

He examined me internally to be quite sure. He said quite definitely that I am like that, so I suppose I can begin to prepare for the great occasion, which I do sincerely hope will be alright.

It has been well worth waiting for and God has answered our prayers after all. I expect you will be very

thrilled about the news, love, at the prospect of being
made a father of your offspring.

[From George]

Potter Hanworth
[Early September]

Darling, I can't tell you in writing how pleased I was this
morning, when I read your letter. It's the best news,
dearest, that I could wish for.

It has relieved your mind, hasn't it, love, to know that
everything is alright, so don't worry, and take care of
yourself, dearest. I know that there are some anxious times
ahead until it's over, but with God's blessing, all will be
well.

I've offered up many little prayers while we've been
waiting for it to be certified, love. Darling, I shall be with
you on Tuesday, so we shall be able to talk it over between
ourselves.

[From Nan]

At Mary's
17 November

It's a lovely moonlight night, and as I came down the
road, I thought of the happy nights we used to spend
across the meadows on the stile. Do you remember, when
we were courting? What happy times they were, love,
when you look back, and what vast changes since then.

However, I hope we have got over the worst days and
it won't be long before the better days are here and I shall
have you to share the happy times with me and the little
newcomer.

Don't worry about me, as I feel much better today.
I'm sure to have my off-days. Dolly and I have finished the
little coats and, really, they look beautiful, George, now
mother has finished putting the final touches to them. You
know what a fidget she is. She put some lovely blue
ribbon through the one that Dolly made. I'm going to do

just another little white one and then, I think, I've finished them. Nora has done for me two pairs of lovely little slippers and she's making a coat now. I shan't be short of anything, I don't think, and mother has nearly finished my other silk cushion cover.

At Mary's
19 November

I'm feeling a bit better than I did when I wrote to you on Monday, but I don't feel as well as I did when I was first carrying my baby. I have rather restless nights, for one thing. I get cramp in my legs and sometimes my back is awful. I suppose, though, I shan't feel so well now as the time goes on. I wouldn't mind so much if I could get more rest in the daytime, but Dad won't give his work up at all.

That would make it a bit easier. You see, when you have to do everything and answer the door all the time, it doesn't give one much peace.

However, I will wait until you have your next leave and then I shall get you to bring some of my things down to Mary's for me, so that I can stay altogether and I shan't be a nuisance up at home till I have my baby, anyway.

At Mary's
27 November

Love, the Nurse is very busy bringing babies into the world, I can tell you, and they are nearly all little boys. She's got fifteen before Xmas and she told us on Tuesday that she hadn't been to bed since the Thursday before. She was tired out. I hope when I have my baby that she isn't so busy if I do have it at home. She is always so funny when she's overtired and worked like that.

At Mary's
15 December

It's very mild for the time of year. It doesn't seem seasonal for nearly Christmas. It won't be much of a Xmas, though, will it? People can't enjoy themselves, I'm sure, when there is all this unrest going on in the world. It makes you wonder sometimes if this time next year it will be the same. You can't imagine what it will be like to live happily again. I know it must seem awful to you, love, as each year keeps slipping by.

What a difference it would make if this war was over and all of you were at home, where you ought to be. But according to the wireless, there has got to be a lot of sacrifice yet in the way of lives going West.

It seems so wicked when you think about it all, and all for the sake of money and greed. I'm sure everybody is fed up with it all, but I hope and pray this time next year it will be a peaceful world we live in.

It was wicked how all those little children got killed in London last week, wasn't it? Such innocent little beings, and all someone's little loved ones. You don't have children to be taken from you like that, do you? Those relatives won't forgive the Jerries very soon, will they?

1943

[From George]

Potter Hanworth
14 January

Love, did you see in the Sunday paper where a little baby
met its death in one of those utility prams through it not
having any brakes? Not that I want to persuade you to
have the other one, but we shall have to have something to
act as a brake if you have a new one, darling.

c/o Greenland Farm
Caen Hill
Gt Limber
Lincolnshire
21 January

Darling, I'm writing again, but when we shall get any
letters, the Lord above knows. We seem to be cut off from
the rest of the world out here.

　Well, dearest, how are you keeping these days? I'm
anxiously waiting for my next leave, darling. What a leave
that will be, to come and see you with our little treasure.
I'm sure it will be the greatest moment of my life.

　I'm lost without hearing from you, but I know it's
not your fault. The post is very bad round these parts. You
will notice the change of address, pidge. It's the nearest
farm to us, so we are having the letters sent there, instead
of going right into the village for them.

[From Nan]

At Mary's
14 February

Well, love, the Dr's been to examine me today, and he
says everything's in order and I shouldn't go above
another fortnight before my baby is born. He told mother

he wants to be with me when it is born, so she mustn't be afraid to send for him, no matter what happens.

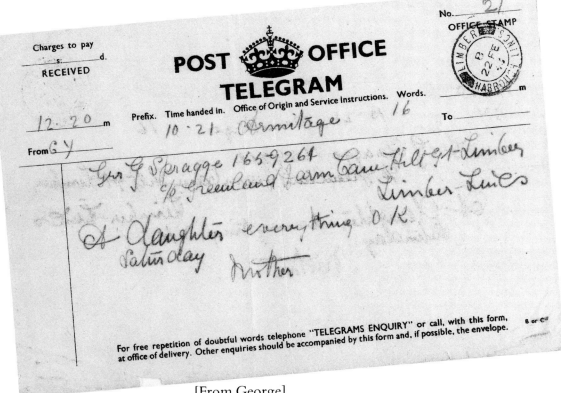

POST OFFICE TELEGRAM

[From George]

Greenland Farm
1 March

I'm sorry, dearest, that I broke down, but really, love, I never was so cut up in my life as I was yesterday. I feel a little better now I'm back, but I'm thinking of you both all the time, darling.

I was on guard at 2 and my thoughts were with you and our little treasure. Darling, God presented us with a lovely child and gave you the strength to bear it. I thank him for it every night.

She's a grand little girl, isn't she, love? I'm not a bit disappointed that it wasn't a boy, darling.

Take care of yourself and don't try to rush matters. Give little Dorothy a hug and kiss for her Dad and God bless you both.

[From Nan]

Swan Inn
3 March

I thought about you many a time, love, and I felt so lonely
after you had gone.

I'm feeling much better in myself, love, I'm pleased to
tell you, and our little Dorothy is going on splendid. She
has had two very good nights these last two nights and I
am able to manage to feed her myself without having to
give her any extra milk. She is coming on beautifully, so I
think my milk must be suiting her alright.

[From George's mother]

Red Brook Lane
10 March

Dear Son
We went to Armitage on Sunday. Little Dorothy had been
for her first walk. She gets wide awake with her blue eyes.

Mary heard from Les yesterday. He says you have
proved a man and he will try when he comes home. I
wonder when it will be.

[From Nan]

Swan Inn
[Mid March]

My word, love, there won't have to be any slips made, as I
wouldn't like to think I'd got to go through that lot for a
few years. You will see a difference in me when you come
again, I can tell you. It seems to have altered me quite a lot
and made me bend a bit.

I expect I shall soon be going to be Churched so that I
can go out for a little walk somewhere. [This refers to the
Church of England 'Churching of Women', prayers of
thanksgiving for a safe delivery. In Staffordshire it was
thought 'unlucky' for a woman to be admitted to a home

141

*George enjoying home leave
with Nan and Dorothy.*

until she had been churched – a throwback to superstitions about purification after childbirth, rituals which still took place as late as the 1960s. Nan evidently felt the streets of Armitage would be contaminated if she walked them unchurched.]

I shall be glad when this rotten lot is over so we can have a home of our own and a bit of home comforts. Sometimes I think it will last a long time yet.

When you look at the papers, they are talking about 1945. It doesn't seem natural, does it, to be away from each other all the time?

Swan Inn
[Mid March]

I have been to be churched this morning. Nora went with me and we had Holy Communion afterwards, so it was very nice, wasn't it? The Rector fetched me in the car and brought me back. It was very kind of him, wasn't it?

Mother has just come in from the fowl, so I expect I shall soon be upstairs as I don't have the baby downstairs when we are open at night. When I am at Mary's I shall be able to let her cry when she wants to. It's rotten with the bar being open all the time. You know what it is like here.

[From George]

Greenland Farm
28 August

Those washdays about knock you out, don't they, love? I should be inclined to make two lots of it, but I suppose you like to get it done and put away.

I'm pleased you had a nice time at Brereton, love, and I'm glad that Dorothy was well enough to go. I'm longing to see her little teeth, pidge. I try to picture her smiling so you can see them. I bet she does look sweet.

Greenland Farm
19 November

I'm just longing to get home to see you both again,
darling. This time next week I shall have had the pleasure
of putting our little treasure in her cot.

[The letter from Nan which provoked this unusual display
of irritation from George is one of the few that have not
survived. Of the 2,000 letters that remain, this is the only
one in which George loses his temper with his wife.]

Greenland Farm
23 December

Darling, I received your letter this morning and I'm very
pleased to hear that Dorothy is a little better. I hope her
cold will soon leave her, but if she's cutting so many teeth
I expect it will hang on for a while, love.

Now, regarding the letter. I was very surprised when
I read it, pidge. You seem to think I don't know where my
responsibilities lie. I don't think you had any cause to
grumble during the last four leaves I've had and I'm
prepared to have Dorothy when I do come home.

You know it's not my fault I'm in this darned lot as
well as I do. No-one would be more pleased than me to be
home for good.

I know how you feel, love, but I'll have her when I
come and you can have a whole week's rest from mauling
with her. I do know how weary you must feel, having
Dorothy all on your own, and I do feel sorry for you. But
you can rest assured I'll do my best to give you a break
when I come on the 3rd, dearest.

I've been on duty throughout the night and I'm on
tomorrow from 4 till midnight, so I shall have a pleasant
Christmas Eve!

We've bought two live cocks from the farm for
Christmas. They are beauties, over 16 pounds the two, so
we shall be alright for something to eat.

Well, dearest, I haven't got a lot of news for you.
Only cheer up, love, you ought to know how much I love
you both.

*Emma Scragg (George's
mother) with Dennis
Meacham and Dorothy.*

143

Some members of George's squad in the Scots Guards, autumn 1944; George [back right] told Nan he was the 'daddy of the group'. Stan Middleton is back left.

George's transfer form which moved him from the Northamptonshire Regiment (where he did infantry training in 1944) to the Scots Guards.

Mrs. J. Scragg

Pay Form 23
This portion only
to be gummed to
Army Form D440T

FROM THE REGIMENTAL PAYMASTER,
ARMY FORM D.440.T.
Army Pay Office,
Regt.
129-137, Marylebone Road,
LONDON, N.W.1.

Sir or Madam,

Number) 1659264 (Rank) Gds. (Name) Scragg G.

...been transferred from Northants Regt. to Scots Gds. ...sequently, all matters affecting your Army Allowance will be dealt with by this office.

It is important that the name and address of the Regimental Paymaster shown on your ...wance Order book/s be altered at once. For this purpose please find attached (at side) 2 ... gummed labels. These should be affixed as follows :—

1

Delete
as
necessary

(a) Please gum one label over the address of the present Regimental Paymaster shown at the top right-hand corner of the cover of your Allowance Order Book. The position the label should take is indicated by dotted lines.

(b) Please gum one label over the address on the back of the Life Certificate post-card (Army Form D.440.A or D440W) which you will find amongst the orders at the back of the book. The position the label should take is indicated by dotted lines.

(c) Please gum one label upon the cover of your SUPPLEMENTARY Allowance Book in a position similar to that of the label affixed to your Allowance Order Book.

(d) Please gum the remaining two labels to the covers of your two SUPPLEMENTARY Allowance Books, in positions similar to that of the label affixed to your Allowance Order Book.

When this has been done, please tear off and complete the form below (Part 2) and post it—no stamp is required.

Date 7. 6. 44

B.H. Robinson Capt.

For the Regimental Paymaster.

Chapter Nine

'IF I HAD MY WAY'

George, 1944

In early 1944, with preparations for the invasion of Europe under way, George was one of many thousands of bewildered soldiers scooped up by the army for infantry training. In the way of all armies and all wars, the men knew nothing of the reasons for the disruption. They were shifted to another place, sifted, assessed, re-assigned and moved on. On 2 March 1944, George's service as a Gunner came to an end. He was transferred as a private to the Northamptonshire Regiment for infantry training.

Militia Camp
Tuxford
Nottinghamshire
[Early February]

Well, darling, I really don't know how to begin writing this letter as I feel rather down and there's such a lot of mystery about this move. We don't seem to know anything definite, love.

I didn't know a thing about it until late yesterday. It came as a big surprise to me. There's 22 of us come out of our battery. I believe we are here for three weeks to a month, but I can't be sure. Some are for the Royal Army Service Corps and the others for infantry. I shall do my utmost to keep out of the latter, but don't worry, I shall be OK and take care of myself.

I did think about you on our wedding anniversary. It was the happiest day of my life, love. It's as plain to me as if it was only yesterday and it's five long years ago. Little did we think what lay ahead.

Perhaps it was as well we couldn't see into the future, although we've been as happy as possible, haven't we, dearest? And we've got a lovely little daughter to crown our married bliss. God bless you both. I love you both dearer than life itself.

Tuxford
15 February

There's about eighty going out to sites again tomorrow for ten days and then another lot will go out when they come back. The Medical Officer is giving everyone an exam. I haven't been yet so I don't know how I shall go

on. I might escape going in the infantry. Bob Snoxall is here. He's a decent chap, but single. He doesn't mind where they send him. He's volunteered for the Paratroops, but I'm not volunteering for anything love. I'll go where they decide to send me. We are still in the dark about this move, but time will tell and I'll keep you informed of anything that comes off.

2 Sqd 3 Coy 14 ITC
Northants Regt
Talavera Camp
Northampton
7 March

With being moved about, love, I haven't had a letter yet, but perhaps I shall be having one tomorrow. It seems a long day here, up at ½ past 6 and don't finish till 5 o'clock turned. In some ways it's better than searchlights, but not in others. I think I prefer the old lights, darling, but civvy street would be better than either.

On 19 May 1944, only two weeks before the launching of the D-Day landings by Allied forces on the shores of France, George found himself in the Scots Guards, an elite combat regiment with a long, proud history of honours in the forefront of many battles.

Because of the regiment's reputation, many of the Scots Guards recruits were volunteers, but the scale of the task in the European campaign meant the army had to draft men to provide the numbers necessary to replace casualties among the soldiers already assigned to the invasion. Since George's letters make it quite clear that he would not offer himself, it seems likely that he was simply the right physical type available at a time when the regiment needed a steady stream of men to be ready for the fighting ahead. George Scragg probably ended up in the front line because he was 5 feet 10½ inches tall, physically fit and, above all, obedient.

George's commanding officer in his last days with the Scots Guards, explained, 'We need ordinary men, stable personalities, men who will do as they are told without question. Aggressive types cause problems and make life

147

uncomfortable for those around them. Men endure in battle because they have pride in their regiment and because they do not want to let their friends down.'

The Guards taught obedience through discipline, drills and standards of 'spit and polish' acknowledged to be among the toughest in any army. Perhaps the ultimate achievement of any efficient army training is that it renders a human being more fearful of the consequences of disobedience that of death itself. Therefore, the enemy may not get you, but you will never escape the wrath of the Sergeant-Major or the contempt of your companions if you fail.

George was welded into a Guardsman by many sweating hours on the drill square at the Guard's training camp in Pirbright in Surrey, and by simulated battle conditions, facing live ammunition and shells on the army's range in the rugged hills of North Wales.

George fell off a lorry in East Anglia and hurt his head; this is his 'excused helmet' note, which was revoked 11 March 1944.

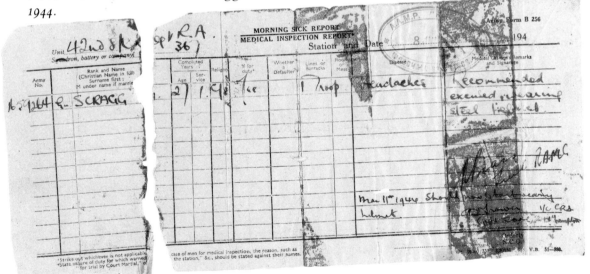

[To Nan's mother]

Scots Guards
Pirbright Camp
Nr Brookwood
Surrey
15 June

Yes, I've got a lot to look forward to in our little Dorothy, bless her. I try to picture her walking about and talking in her little way. I'm missing a lot, aren't I? Still, I suppose we've got to make the best of it and hope and pray that the time isn't far distant when we are all back home again and look on these war years as a bad dream.

Yes, mam, I'll take care of myself as far as I can. It's easy this side of the water, but it's in someone else's hands when you cross into the front line. He alone can bring you through that hell, and my faith and trust will be in Him when the time comes. I'm getting sentimental, aren't I? That won't do.

I know you will be looking after Nan and Dorothy. I'm more than grateful to you and I've got no worries regarding that, but, all the same, they are always topmost in my thoughts.

[To Nan's mother]

Warren Camp
Llandwrog
Nr Caernarvon
North Wales
6 July

I'm alright, but I could do with being home again. Ever since I came through Armitage on Monday I've felt real homesick. To think I was so near to you all and could do nothing about it. I would have given anything just to see Nan and our little Dorothy. I kept a good lookout, but I know it was a thousand to one chance of seeing them. I saw Charlie Brown working on the line. I think I gave him a bit of a shock, but he recognised me alright. We had a straight through run from London, no changing at all.

Well, dear, it's a lovely place, just nice for a holiday, right close to the sea. I can hear the rollers from here and the mountains rear up at the back, but I'm afraid it's no holiday for us. It's a real toughening up we are getting. The food is good, but the huts aren't too comfortable. Still, it could be worse, I suppose.

[To Nan]

Pirbright
[Mid July]

Although I've put the Surrey address on, pidge, I'm still in
Wales, but we are moving off in the morning. I expect I
shall be coming through again, love. Isn't it maddening to
think we shall be just a matter of yards apart and can do
nothing about it? I feel proper upset when I think about it.
I'd love to see you and our little Dorothy, but I know the
chance is very remote. Still, I'll be looking round, love. I'll
have this ready to throw out if I see anyone I know.

We finished the course today. I'm pleased in a way,
for we were always wet through. They found the toughest
spots for the job, pidge, streams, bogs and hills. It's been a
proper test all round.

Pirbright
11 August

Well, darling, I can't tell you how I felt at leaving you and
our little Dorothy. There can never be a worse parting,
dearest, but keep your chin up.

It may not be as black as it appears. It was very hard
to leave you. I can understand fellows deserting at the last
moment, but it does no good. They catch up with you in
the end, so it's just as well to take it as it comes.

I can't give you any information at the moment where
I'm going, pidge. They don't need us all for draft, so it's a
case of waiting for developments.

I saw lots of people along the river banks as I came
back, love. I thought of our little treasure running around
in her little sun suit. I hope you went out. You mustn't
stay in, love, keep going, and I hope this time next year we
shall be enjoying a lovely holiday at St Annes. Although
things look rather dull at the present, this war will soon be
over and then for a lifetime of happiness with our little
treasure. I enjoyed every moment we spent together,
darling. I know we have a few words, but I love you dearer
than life itself. No-one could ever take your place, so take
no notice of the words we have, darling.

I know our love is true. Don't worry, darling, I'll be back with you both before many months have passed.

Special – Darling the officers have just had us together to read out the names who are going and I'm not on it. I think I'm staying here, love, for specialist training.

Pirbright
[Mid August]

Well, darling, there's been another change in the plans. We aren't going up north after all. We were all ready for the move, everything packed, when the Company Commander had us on parade to tell us it had been cancelled. Perhaps it's as well, for it's rumoured that the Batt. we were going to join up there will be for the Far East.

We are moving out on Thurs, love, to one of the large camps, that's if it's not cancelled, prior to going to France. But don't worry, dearest, I'll be alright. I know your thoughts will be with me and mine will be with you and our little treasure.

YMCA
19 August

Well, darling, I'm sorry I couldn't write before, but you will understand how things are in the army, especially now. It's hard to get a letter away, but we've been given time off to get out, so I'm writing this in the canteen. I'm alright, so don't worry, love.

I'm sending my money home, love, as it won't be any use to me, so buy yourself and Dorothy something out of it. It's still uncertain where we are going, but wherever it is, don't worry, I'll take good care of myself and come back to you and the sweetest little girl in the world. I've no address yet, but I'll write as often as I can, darling, so keep smiling. It won't be long now.

George in the Scots Guards, autumn 1944; Nan made him promise to shave his moustache off.

George sent Nan cards from Brussels following its liberation in 1944.

Chapter Ten

'ON FAR DISTANT SHORE'

George, 1944

As George sailed with other reinforcements for France, the British army was reorganising after its heavy losses since D-Day. Between 31 July, and 20 August, when George embarked, the Guards Armoured Division which he was about to join had had 249 men killed, 975 wounded and 176 missing.

Like most of the young men from the nations who fought this war, George had never been abroad before. In an age when the car and aeroplane were still luxuries for the few, his travels had been limited to holidays by the seaside and short journeys by bus or train. For millions like George, horizons broadened dramatically, but their first encounters with a new culture were distorted. They saw people, towns and landscapes as war had changed them.

The letters George wrote on active service contain no bugles, no heroics, no thrilling accounts of battle. Even without the inhibiting shadow of censorship, George was not interested in such things, only in surviving them.

Suddenly, the reluctant soldier who for more than three years had simply marked his letters home 'Thursday afternoon' or 'Sunday morning' began to date his writings properly. It was as though time and the accurate recording of it had become important to him.

Scots Guards
V Sub Unit
34 RHU
101 Reinforcement Group
BLA
24 August

I watched the shores of old England slowly vanishing away and realised more than ever how much we mean to each other, love. It's a funny sensation, but it will be funnier still when I'm watching them coming into sight once more.

The weather is good and you wouldn't tell the difference between the two countries, love. The money here is a bit complicated but I suppose we shall soon get used to it.

We are able to get quite a lot of different things in the way of chocolate, biscuits, etc., and the fags are plentiful. By the way, love, I've started smoking, only occasionally, though.

Keep your chin up, love. It won't be long now.

PS I've made an extra allowance to you, love, 14s a week, so you will know what it is when it comes through.

On 28 August the Guards moved out of Normandy and the armoured columns began a hectic advance across the Seine and Somme rivers. Within five days, George's unit, X Company, now attached to the 1st Battalion Welsh Guards, had been among the first troops to enter both Arras, and, on 3 September, the Belgian capital, Brussels.

No letters from Nan during George's overseas service survive. Soldiers were not encouraged to keep them, in case of capture.

George's role was the timeless part of the infantry soldier, with a few refinements and concessions to mechanised war. Armed with rifle or Bren gun and grenades, and carrying minimum provisions in a backpack, they were transported in lorries as the armoured columns advanced.

Their job was to follow through and tidy up the holes punched by the swift moving tanks. Sometimes, because of weather conditions and the nature of the ground, the foot

soldiers were sent in first to test and face the enemy defences, wriggling forward, crouching, running, darting
from building to building, tree to tree, hole in the ground to
burnt-out vehicle.

Although the fighting men who drove the war
machines – the battleships, the tanks, the bombers – also
died and suffered appalling injuries, it was their machines
that were the target and the weapon. The foot soldier fights
a personal war. He is the weapon, and the flesh and blood
target. His enemy is shooting at him directly, and a human
body dressed only in a coarse wool battledress blouse and
trousers, with just a steel helmet to offer scant protection to
the head, is pitifully vulnerable. And that vulnerability is
the same for the soldier in the Roman legion as for his sons
and grandsons who marched for Napoleon or Kitchener or
Rommel.

At thirty, George was already an 'old man' by infantry
standards. Battle is a task that society usually assigns to
those in their teens and early twenties.

Forty years later, his friend Stanley Middleton said,
'It's a filthy job and we were only kids who were doing it.
No-one who has ever smelled the disgusting smell of war
can forget it – dead people, dead animals, burning build-
ings, smoke, cordite. After the war I put those things in a
box and shut the lid.'

X Coy Scots Guards
Att 1st Batt Welsh Guards
BLA
28 August

From what I've seen of the places we've passed through,
the French people know there's a war on, for many of
them are practically razed to the ground.

Well, love, if you don't hear from me so often, don't
worry, for I'll write as often as possible, but sometimes it
will be difficult.

X Coy
1 September

Things seem strange out here. The language takes some
understanding, but we get to know a few words. The
French people seem very excited about it all. The whole
village turned out at one place with a bit of a band and the
drummer knocked a hole in it in his excitement. The
kiddies run up and down with bottles of wine, offering it
to us, and showers of apples are thrown to us. The Maquis
[French Resistance] are doing a good job. You can see
them bringing in the Jerry prisoners out of the woods and
they give what information they can. I don't think it will
last much longer. I hope not, anyway, for it's about time
everyone was at peace again.

The liberation of Brussels was always to be remembered as
'the happy time' by George and his comrades as they
struggled on through the misery of the autumn and winter
of 1944. In the cold and wet months ahead, they were
warmed by the memory of their delirious welcome by the
citizens of the Belgian capital, who in their eagerness to
greet the troops surrounded men and vehicles until it was
impossible to advance further. Kisses, cheers, singing and
dancing crowds made it seem that everything was possible,
soon, quickly.

The Welsh Guards group reached the *Palais de Justice*
which the retreating Germans had set on fire in an attempt
to destroy Gestapo documents. What the fire failed to
destroy was the Gestapo's hidden wine store in the cellar,
which the Belgians promptly 'liberated' and shared with the
delighted soldiers.

By the time George wrote of Brussels in his next letter
of 16 September, the Welsh group, after a brief rest in the
capital, had headed for the Albert canal and X Company
had fought off a strong German counterattack at Helch-
teren, where Belgian civilians had tended casualties, and
George and his comrades had been in a vicious four-day
battle for the village of Hechtel. At one stage in the Hechtel
hostilities, X Company were cut off, but managed to hold
out to take the village. German losses were 150 dead, 220
wounded and 500 unwounded prisoners. Guards' losses

since 4 September, when they left Brussels, were 113 killed, 405 wounded, 80 missing. The 1st Welsh, including X Company, suffered some of the highest casualties in the division. No wonder George's letter which, typically, mentions none of these hardships, has a wistful quality. He knew the good news was already old news.

X Coy
16 Sept

It's four years today, love, since I joined up. Doesn't it seem a long time to be parted? I never thought it would last so long, still I think it's in its last throes.

We were the first troops to enter Brussels, love, and what a welcome we received. The people simply went crazy for us. It was like living in a dream. They laughed and cried at the same time. They were scenes I'll never forget, I can't explain them on paper. There was no sleep in that city at night. I expect you read about it, though, in the papers. We've been for a bath today. It's a treat to feel clean once more, I can tell you.

On 21 September, the Welsh Guards group joined the advance to Nijmegen as cover for the evacuation of paratroop survivors of the disastrous Arnhem landings, which had been intended to shorten the war. George's unit were patrolling and in action, repelling counterattacks. By the end of September and early October, the division were at rest south of Nijmegen, having lost 126 killed, with 525 wounded and 80 missing, since the Arnhem rescue began.

X Coy
28 September

The weather is rotten. I wish it was summer instead of winter that was coming. There isn't much to look forward to at this time of year.

The Dutch people don't seem so enthusiastic in their welcome, but they will give you almost anything. We get plenty of fruit, milk and an egg occasionally.

157

X Coy
4 October

According to your letter, Dorothy gets a young nib, but
I'm pleased you are firm with her. She'll soon lose those
ways as she grows up. I can picture her making up to you
after one of her turns. She's got a way with her, I know, of
getting in favour again.

The civilians out here had a poor time under Jerry,
some worse than others. I think it was the poorer class that
felt it worst, but all seem pleased to be free once more.

When we were coming through, our chocolate and
toffee ration went to the kiddies. You should have seen
their faces light up when you gave them some.

I look at the photo many a time and give you both a
kiss. Keep smiling, dearest. I hope we shan't be parted for
much longer.

X Coy
7 October

Darling, I was pleased to hear from you. I had a letter
yesterday and one today. When you get a letter from home
things seem a lot brighter. It's the only bright spot to look
forward to out here.

I like to hear what's going on regarding you both. It
gives me something to build a picture on and I do picture
you both many a time, or try to.

I picture you at home at nights around the fire, having
a chat when the kiddies are in bed. I know I'll make a fuss
of home when I get back after this lot, especially if we are
lucky and soon get one to ourselves, love.

You say you don't know where I am, love. Well, I'm
in Holland, across the Rhine, but it's called the Waal as it
flows into this country. We are in the front, but we get to
know very little of what's going on elsewhere. You at
home have more idea of what's going on than us. There's
been a huge force of bombers over today. I expect they are
softening Jerry up for the next assault.

George's reluctance to explain what was happening to him and his almost romantic picturing of the daily doings of his family while he was in the front line was a very common reaction, according to his comrade, Stan Middleton.

'We weren't allowed to give details, but, in any case, we didn't want our families to know what was happening to us. We didn't want them to understand. We were doing a job that we never could have imagined before, a disgusting job. It helped us to think of our families living a life that was normal, not like ours. And, besides, just knowing we were there, the people at home had enough to worry about.'

X Coy
11 October

I'm very pleased to hear that Lew Rosson got back from Arnhem. It was a great pity we couldn't get through to them in time. We did our best. I think another six hours of daylight on that day and we should have made it, but Jerry was very strong and fanatical up there. We all had a rough passage, I can tell you, love.

We are enjoying a few days out of the line. It's quite a change from being up in the front. We've been doing a bit of drill and PT just to keep our hand in.

Love, I haven't seen any kiddies that look really well. In fact they all seem very undernourished, no Dorothys or Davids out here, and their legs look so thin, especially if they are wearing big wooden clogs.

X Coy
15 October

I went to a picture show last night to see *The Sky's the Limit*, but I'm looking forward to the days when I'm taking you again, love.

It still seems to drag on, doesn't it? Although Jerry must see it's useless. What his idea is I don't know, for it means only destruction for his cities and death for the civilians. Aachen is a typical example of what is in store for them.

Yes, pidge, it was a great sight in Brussels. Anyone

159

there will never forget it. It was on the newsreel at the pictures last night and it took me back to the brighter side of this advance, for I can tell you it hasn't been all 'flowers and fruit' since then. There's been scenes that will live longer in my mind than even Brussels, but that's another story.

X Coy
17 October

At the moment we are in a barn and it's overrun with mice. But there is one consolation, the hens come and lay a few eggs each day. I've just had one for my tea and I did enjoy it, for it's a long time since I had one. The food is good, but we get just enough to keep us hungry, still, we could be worse off, I suppose, love.

X Coy
22 October

We are still out of the line. I could stick this for long enough. I know it can't last for ever, but it's a good break all the same. I went to the pictures yesterday morning and a rugby match during the afternoon, but I don't understand the game much.

I'm pleased Ted is alright. I wouldn't mind being back with them [in Belgium]. They are fairly safe there, but someone has got to be forward, so I trust in God to bring me safely through. I've said a prayer many a time when things have been pretty rough and I've got through, so I hope and pray I always shall. I've only one ambition and that's to get back safely to you and our little treasure. I don't mind what I go through as long as I'm spared.

I'm very pleased to hear that our Dorothy is so intelligent, love. It's a great thing in life to have your wits about you and I hope we have the pleasure of seeing her get on in life.

I know how keen you are on seeing her go to High School. I am for that matter if she has really got the brains, but I don't think anything of sending children to those places if they haven't got it in them, love.

X Coy
24 October

We are still in the old barn, love, plenty of mice to keep us company and the hens have ceased to come in now, so there's no more eggs for anyone. I had two while they did come in.

I went to a picture show yesterday, *This Happy Breed*. Not a bad show at all, love. I also had a bath, but it's getting cold for those sort of things. Still, it makes you feel different again after it.

So the officer has confirmed that Harry was killed in action. It's hard for those that are left, but, as you say, there are hundreds the same. Old Jerry plasters his mortar bombs down thick and fast when he does start. I've gone through some and they're very uncomfortable. You laugh afterwards, but it's no laughing matter at the time, pidge.

X Coy
29 October

I expect you will be busy knitting for the liberated people at nights now, love, but don't overdo yourself with it, for you can do with plenty of rest.

I should have thought before now of asking you to send some woollens out, love, scarf, balaclava and gloves, for I guess we shall be needing them before long and it will take a week or so to get here. Will you make a parcel up for me, darling? The old things will do fine, and put some toothpaste in too, pidge. We've been issued with our winter pants and vests, but I don't expect we shall get comforts like we did in Searchlights.

It will soon be three months since I last saw you, darling. When I look back and think it seems years. I miss you more than ever, dearest. You are always in my thoughts and prayers. Take care of yourself, keep smiling and don't worry overduly.

X Coy
1 November

We aren't in the line yet, but we've moved out of the old barn to some very good billets, electric lights, wash basins and we've a wireless to entertain us, so we are very well off at the moment. But the bed isn't so comfortable as it was on the straw.

About six of us went out this afternoon to have a look round the place, but there's nothing to buy, so we went to a film show, Bing Crosby in *Going My Way*. He's a great singer, isn't he?

I enjoyed reading your letter. It gives me a good idea of what our Dorothy is like with her little ways. I hope she hasn't grown out of them before I'm with you both again, darling. She's coming on well with her talking, isn't she? And according to your letter, she's very knowing and understands well what you say, bless her little heart.

I *do* miss you both so much. Every day seems worse, but I look at it like this, it's one day nearer the end of this war and the sooner it's over, the quicker we shall be together, darling.

X Coy
3 November

I'm doing my best to write a letter, but it's on my knee. One chap's singing, or trying to, I should say, and another's blowing on a mouth organ, so I hope you will be able to read it alright, pidge.

We've moved out of billets, but don't worry, we aren't in the thick of things yet, darling.

Well, dearest, it will be eleven years by day and by date on Sunday since I first took you home. It doesn't seem that long, does it, love? I get mixed up with some dates, but I can remember that one.

X Coy
9 November

I expect Ted finds it a lot different now he is moving about
and under canvas. But it's better than this life, all the same,
stuck in a trench, mud everywhere and wet through most
of the time. Anyone who hasn't experienced it has no idea
what it's like, but as long as I pull through I don't mind
what I go through. It's been snowing this morning, but
it's cleared up again now.

The officer told me one of my letters to you had been
destroyed by a shell, so if you are a few days without a
letter, you will understand, love.

X Coy
13 November

Darling, I'm sorry I haven't been able to write to you these
last few days, but now we are back to civilisation once
again. The weather is something awful out here. I hope
you are having better or the kiddies will be tormenting
you indoors and I know what that means.

We just did a week up the line and what a week it was.
No wash or shave. Talk about wild men, it wasn't in it,
and the trenches were ankle deep in water. I was never so
fed up in my life, pidge. Still, we have to grin and bear it, I
suppose.

We had plenty to eat as we were round about some
farms and, of course, they were deserted, so the fowl,
rabbits and a few pigs helped the rations out a bit.

There's no end of cattle lying dead in the fields, killed
by shells, and they don't half smell. There was one a few
yards from our trench and it was stinking the place out and
we couldn't do anything about it as they are no little things
to bury. We miss the fruit these days, but we had our share
when there was some, love.

No wonder the speed of advance has slowed down.
All the fields are under water. No tanks can operate in such
country. If only we had summer instead of winter, I don't
think it would last much longer.

X Coy
14 November

I'm alright, pidge, just lying back again taking things
cushy after our week up the line. We've got a roof over
our heads and electric light, so we are quite comfortably
off.

It's an awful night, snowing and raining. I've just
come off guard, but I've still got another spell to do, worse
luck.

I think it will be another Xmas that we shan't spend
together. The kiddies are just at that age when they could
do with us at home, still, there are thousands the same, so
make it as happy a time as you can for them.

How is your Dad keeping? Remember me to him,
love. Tell him I'm looking forward to having a drink with
him before next 'muck spreading time'.

They've just dished out the rum ration, love. It isn't
much, but it warms up the cockles a bit.

X Coy
17 November

The weather is colder than ever today. It was a sharp frost
during the night. I was very thankful the parcel had
arrived, for it was darned cold in the trenches. Don't think
I'm in the front line with being in trenches, darling. As a
matter of fact, we only man them at night, just as a
precautionary measure. We have billets during the day, so
we are really well off, don't you think so, pidge?

The last week we were up at the front was just over
the border into Jerry country, so I've been over the line.
But I might tell you it was warm up there. He just churned
the ground up with his shelling. Luckily, he didn't hit any
of the trenches.

Mind you, he was too close to be comfortable, it was
only a matter of feet in a good many cases and it would
have spelt finish for a good many.

The officer had a close one. It destroyed the mail for
us. One or two suffered from shock, but no-one was
injured.

There seems to be a big push just starting, according

to the wireless, love. I hope it's *the* one that will see the job over.

I think it will be my turn to walk out tomorrow, so I'll have another good search for something for you and Dorothy. I should like to send you something for a souvenir, darling, for I know you would treasure something from here.

X Coy
18 November

It's a lovely day after a real wet night. I was pleased when morning came round, for there wasn't much rest as everything was wet through. It was like sleeping under a tap, drip, drip, drip, all the time. It's a treat to get back to the billets, love.

The wireless is going. 'Music while you work' is on now. It cheers the place up quite a lot and it's nice to have the news. I've just been spud peeling for dinner, but there was plenty on the job, so it didn't take long.

I'm sorry to hear our Dorothy is so masterful. I think if you let David hit her back it will cure her of those sort of tricks. Poor little chap, I bet he would cry. But all the same I had to smile when I read about it. I could just picture her in the act.

X Coy
20 November

I've managed to get you and Dorothy a Christmas present, love. I packed it off this morning and I hope you get it safely and before Christmas. I was fortunate to get a doll. It isn't what I should have liked, but it was the best there was, love. I'd just come in with the doll when I received your letter saying that our little treasure said Santa was bringing her a dolly. Bless her, I hope she will love it and get it in time for Xmas. I only wish that I could be home, darling. It does get me at times when I think about it.

I also got a jigsaw puzzle which might amuse David. It's all I could get for him, love. It's a problem to buy anything out here. The Battalion got them to sell to the

165

troops and there was hardly anything left when this company went up.

I got you a pair of silk stockings, but not from there, love. It was a bit of black marketing to get them. I hope you like them, love. I got you a bottle of scent, too.

The 'black market' flourished all over Europe, wherever rationing had made certain goods scarce, and therefore highly desirable. Although the exchange and barter of negotiable commodities like chocolate, cigarettes, and silk or nylon stockings was strictly illegal, in many countries on the continent they became the only reliable form of payment because the currencies were so unstable. George's Christmas parcel of silk stockings and perfume represented considerable treasure to his wife in an England starved of luxuries. The fact that the officer who censored George's letter allowed not only the deal but evidence of it to pass shows the extent to which the system had become accepted.

The precious scent that George bought on the blackmarket for Nan, and the duty-free form he needed to get it to her; she kept it in the original box, and traces of scent remain today.

166

X Coy
29 November

We've changed around the billets again. We are back to the
first place we came to with a nice radiator and electric
light. I think it's the best place.

But Jerry gets us on our toes at times with his
shelling. They are bursting pretty close at the moment, the
debris is falling round us. I hope he doesn't get any closer.
We don't pay a lot of notice to them though, as we've had
plenty of experience.

X Coy
1 December

Three of our section have gone to an investiture today. I
don't know how many decorations this Coy is getting for
the Hechtel affair, but there is quite a few, I believe. I don't
think we shall ever get it as rough as it was there, love.

We had the old NAAFI van round yesterday and got
a few fags, soap, biscuits and a bar of chocolate, so we
didn't do so bad. I might go to the pictures at the Div.
Club this afternoon. I got ready to go this morning, but
somehow I got left with the billet to clean up, so it was too
late.

X Coy
5 December

We have been moved out of our billets among the civvy
houses as Jerry got to know where we were. One of our
fellows was killed and another injured when a shell burst
through the roof, so they decided to scatter us about a bit.
It's a good job it happened at night when the majority had
gone to their trenches or, no doubt, there would have been
a lot more casualties, love.

There's five of us at the moment, busy writing letters
in the sitting room. It's a lovely house, everything up to
date, but they make us very welcome. Nothing's too
much trouble for them. It makes me feel a bit homesick,
love, but all the same, it's nice.

The woman has just brought us a grand cup of coffee each and 'Music while you work' is on the wireless. It's like heaven after the times we've had, love.

I'm pleased you got the photos alright, love. As you say, I would look strange with a moustache, but it will come off before I come home.

Yes, they are all young fellows, ranging from 19 to 23. I'm the daddy of them all. The one at the back of the group with me is the one I pair up with when we are in the trenches. He's a nice fellow, no silliness about him and keeps a cool head up at the front. It's better when you have somebody who doesn't dither in the trench with you. If you get dug in with somebody who does, you are as bad yourself in no time, love.

This letter and the photograph introduced George's family to his best friend in the Scots Guards, a young Yorkshireman called Stanley Middleton.

Stan, who had worked as a draughtsman, had, as he put it, 'sneaked off' to avoid upsetting his mother, to sign on as a volunteer. Born in Barnsley, Stan came, like George, from a coalmining community. Although younger, Stan was more experienced in battle than George, being a veteran of the Guards Armoured Division campaign, which began at the end of June 1944 with the vicious battles for the Normandy countryside.

'George was a wonderful man,' Stan recalled, 'a God-fearing, clean-living man. I never saw him drunk or chasing women. I never heard him grumble. He was cheerful to be with and had a really naughty sense of humour. When we were sleeping in the old barn, he teased me all night about the mice and rats coming to get me. Christ Stan, he said, there's a real big one over there and it's coming this way.'

Stan clearly remembered George describing hilariously to his incredulous young companions the functions of the bidet – which he pronounced 'biddy' – then a rare sight in a British bathroom.

'We were all saying what we had done before the war and George said, "I make bidets." We were kids, we'd never been anywhere before we'd been in the Army, and when he told us what they were for, we couldn't stop laughing. We didn't believe him.

Stan sent this picture to Nan in late 1944.

169

'I liked to hear him talk. His accent fascinated me. I'd never heard anyone speak in that dialect before. He was my best friend. We watched out for each other, shared things and slept together. It wasn't homosexual, it was practical. You could share your blankets and keep warmer.'

Although George was an unwilling soldier, said Stan, he always did his best. 'He wasn't interested in the army, or in the war, really. I never remember discussing with him what it was about. All he wanted was to do what he had to do, get the job finished and go home.'

X Coy
12 December

I spent a nice 48 hrs leave in Brussels, pidge. I didn't think the army would go to so much trouble in catering for us. There's no doubt about it, everything was tip-top.

We are in a ten-storey hotel. There was a bedroom for each one, with wash basin, wardrobe, electric lights and a real lovely bed in each.

The latest time for breakfast was ½ past 9. I just made it the first morning, but it was after ten when I woke today, on my back with my arms behind my head, just like our little Dorothy lies. I did enjoy the rest, love.

Brussels is a lively city and the shops are pretty well stocked. But, oh dear, the price of everything. When we first went in they would have given you anything, but it's up another street now, love. I've bought you a fountain pen. I've heard you say you would like one, so I'll be sending it, darling, one of the days.

We reported back to our own billets only to find that the Coy has moved, so we are spending a night in a transit camp before joining them tomorrow. I went to the civvy house where we were billeted only to find our lads had gone and another lot there.

The people soon made me some tea, boiled an egg and wanted me to stay the night there, but of course, I couldn't. They don't like those that are billeted on them now.

They gave me their address to write to them. They are really a very nice family, very religious, RC, of course. There's a figure of the Virgin Mary on a shelf with a cross that is lit up the whole of the time. Their son has been to college and speaks five different languages. I really enjoyed my stay with them. When we came in off the night on guard, they wanted us to go to their beds, but of course we didn't. But it goes to show how welcome we were, love.

[To Nan from Minnie Middleton (Stan's mother)]

Staincross
Barnsley
13 December 1944

Dear Mrs Scragg
Your husband and my son are together in Holland doing their job side by side and I thought I would like to write to you. Stan writes me they are very good friends and I am very glad to know. He is only young but I feel that he has the comradeship of an older person. I had a group photograph sent from Stan with the 5 men of their squad and he says what a happy family they are. You will be as glad to know about that as myself.

Perhaps you will have heard from your husband of the proud day of their investiture with Monty. I have searched the newspapers hoping to find some pictures but haven't found any so far.

But what we are most wanting is our men and boys and we look forward to that time to be not far hence. News seems very good at the moment and we feel sure that there will be peace on earth and good will towards men very soon.

Stan does not mention if you have any family. I should love to have a few lines from you, dear, anytime.

[From George]

X Coy
18 December

I'm alright, pidge, back out of it again for a while. With going to Brussels I wasn't up the line as long as the others, so I was rather lucky going when I did, love.

171

However, it wasn't so bad. We had plenty to eat, plenty of fowl and a few pigs. All civilians had been moved out of the village, so we did all the cooking ourselves in the houses. And what a mess the places got in during our stay, but it didn't matter much as it was a German village.

Old Jerry gets rather active at nights with his planes. They seemed to be following us out last night. The searchlights caught one in their beams and the guns soon brought it down. It crashed about 400 yrds from us in flames.

On 16 December 1944, the Germans launched a big counter-offensive in the Ardennes. Although the greatest impact was in the sector manned by United States troops, as they temporarily reeled from the shock, the whole front was affected by the onslaught. The Guards Armoured Division, which had been due for relief, was ordered to cover the River Meuse, between Namur and Huy.

X Coy
20 December

It's been a very foggy day, a real pea-souper. It would be a good job if we could have a few nice days so that the rocket firing planes could get amongst Jerry's armour that he's thrown against the Yanks. He seems to have hit back pretty hard, according to the wireless.

Those who have been over here six months drew for their turn to go home on leave today. My mate Stan drew number 39, so he should be going on the 8th of Feb, that's if there's no alteration in the scheme.

By the way, love, he must have been mentioning me in his letters home, for he told me his mother will be very likely writing to you.

X Coy
24 December

I was surprised when you said that you had heard from
Stan's mother so soon. He had a letter saying his mother
has heard from you, so it looks like you having someone
else to correspond with. It's nice to have someone to kind
of talk things over with, especially as we are together in
this lot. I hope both of you keep it up and I think you will.

Old Jerry has staged a comeback hasn't he? But I
think he's being slowed down now. If that lot can be held
and wiped out I don't think it will be long before it's over.
It may be his last effort, it looks that way to me.

We are well to the rear of it at present, billeted again
in civvy houses. But where we are the people haven't any
coal and the floor is quarries, so it's very cold to sleep on.
Stan and two more of the section have got stomach pains. I
think it's the cold that has struck them.

I'm sure today is the coldest we have had. I was on
guard last night and, with no fire for us to come in to, I
was absolutely starved.

It's a grand day for the airforce. I can hear them going
over. They are the boys to steady up Jerry with their
rockets and bombs.

No, love, I don't think I've any more to add to what
I've told you about Brussels. I had a nice quiet time. Mind
you, it's the same there as any other city in Europe, you
can be led astray if you are that way inclined. But you
know, dearest, I'm not interested in anyone but you. Not
if I was out here years would I do anything like that, love.
[Nan's worries were not entirely the product of her
imagination, although they were unfounded as far as
George was concerned. Many Allied soldiers contracted
venereal disease on their leaves out of the line.]

Jerry sends his flying bombs. You can hear them
chugging over at nights. The ack-ack shot two down close
by here last night, but they exploded in midair.

It's a little out of the way place we are now, love, very
little life about. They are nearly all farmers and some queer
ways they have of carting their stuff about. You see a
horse and a cow harnessed together or a couple of bullocks
dragging a cart. It all seems strange, nothing up to date at
all.

Late on Christmas Eve, orders came for the Welsh Guards group, to which X Company was still attached, to move forward. They reached Namur early on Christmas morning and took up position on high ground. All special rations had to be left behind and it was no consolation to the unhappy soldiers of X Company that the town of Namur was the scene of their regiment's first battle honour. They spent a miserable Christmas being bombed by the Germans, until they were relieved on 27 December, when they had a belated Christmas dinner.

The interesting aspect of George's reaction to this is its restraint. Where before he would be likely to complain about the injustice of it all, he now shrugs it off as one of those things a soldier must tolerate. Although he does not like the army any more than he did at the beginning, combat seems to have made him more understanding and more accepting of its foibles.

X Coy
29 December

We thought we were going to have a nice little time. All the fare had arrived at HQ, cake, puddings, drink etc. But it wasn't to be for orders came at midnight to pack up ready to move off early morning, so Xmas Day was spent on the journey.

There was plenty of cursing going on, but that doesn't make things any better. We just have to take it, but all the same, it was vexing, pidge. I'm pleased to say we are back again in the same village and hoping to have our Christmas here.

It was a rotten place we went to, out in the wilds, no fires, and it was terribly cold. We wasn't sorry to get back here, love. The cake was the only reminder that it was Xmas.

Love, I'm looking forward to having a letter from you telling me all about our little Dorothy's Christmas. I do hope you all had a good time and there was no little tears. My thoughts were with you all the time, darling. I expect they were both up early to see what Santa had brought them. I should have loved to have been there.

I expect the bar was the usual rowdy place. Did

Captain get up to give them a few songs? I don't think the old times will come back again, love.

It's terribly foggy today, pidge. There won't be much air activity in this lot, but the last few days allowed the airforces to deal Jerry some smashing blows. No doubt about it, they are the lads who are playing a big part in this war. I hope the weather picks up again so they can carry on with the good work.

X Coy
30 December

Well, dearest, we had our Christmas yesterday, and it was quite a good do, considering there is so many to cater for. I think everybody enjoyed themselves. Of course, there was the usual few that went too far, but I suppose it's their way of enjoying themselves, getting the worse for drink.

There was plenty to eat, for once there was food left over. And there was wine, beer and rum for everybody, so I don't think we did amiss. Oh, and an orange each too.

Love, the leave to England has started, so I expect you will be having some of the village lads home. One of our section goes on the 5th. I don't know how long it will be before I come. I hope they step up the quota in between times or it will be months yet.

I think they have sized up Jerry's offensive. It won't be long before he's being rolled back with a sore head. The airforce played a big part in bringing him to a halt.

Stan and I went for a bath today. It's about five or six weeks since we had one, so I think we needed it, don't you, love?

In the event of my death I give the whole of my property and effects to my wife Mrs Florence Annie Scragg ℅ Swan Inn: Armitage: Staffs:

Signature *George Scragg*

Rank and Regiment *Gdsn. Scots Guards*

Army Number *165926k*

Date *17th August. 1944*

Books 64 (Part 1)/2.
Wt. 24596/B.68.   920M.   10/43.   J&SLtd.   51-7331.

George's will.

176

Chapter Eleven

'THE DAYS DWINDLE DOWN'

George, 1945

By the middle of January 1945, the Allied counterattack had eliminated the German salient in the Ardennes, which the Americans had christened 'The Bulge'. In the early days of the New Year, George and his companions found themselves once more billeted with hospitable Belgian families while they went through another round of training and exercises in preparation for the next offensive. One more operation, they were told, and X Company would rejoin their own regiment, when the 1st Battalion Welsh Guards would be replaced by the 2nd Battalion Scots Guards.

X Coy
1 January

They look on New Year's Day as a Sunday here and the woman invited us in to tea this afternoon. She does everything for us, washes and darns the socks, brings hot coals in to start a fire in the mornings. In fact she makes us very welcome.

There were two great plates of things something like pancakes for us and plenty of coffee and then we had two glasses of white rum each. We quite enjoyed ourselves. Of course, we have difficulty in understanding their language, but still we piece things together and get along OK.

X Coy
5 January

There's a big whist drive in the village hall tonight, but I
haven't gone. I'd rather sit round the bit of fire and write
letters or have a read. I don't enjoy them a bit when it's all
men. Not that I want women, but everything gets
muddled when it's time to move. It's real panicky, love.
I've only been once and it was enough for me.

We do a bit of training these days. It's really better
than lying about getting stale. Yesterday we split up into
fives and went from place to place using the compass only.
It was quite interesting.

There was a prize for the first party in. We got in first,
but the officer said we hadn't had time to do the course.
We did do it. However, it's no good arguing. Old Stan
was quite put out about it.

X Coy
7 January

Well, love, I went out yesterday, but I'm sorry to say I
didn't see anything I could buy. Stan was able to come
too. We went to an ENSA show in the afternoon and
pictures at night. We tried to get something to eat, but
couldn't. Every place was full, regardless of the price of
things, 60 francs for a tea meal, that's above 7 shillings.
And 100 francs for a piece of beef steak. It's really too
much for the likes of Tommies, isn't it?

It's snowing hard at the moment, love. If it keeps on
we shall be snowed up tomorrow. We go out for firing all
day tomorrow and Stan starts on a motor transport
course. I wouldn't mind learning to drive myself. It's
always useful back in civvy life, isn't it?

X Coy
9 January

It's proper winter now outside, plenty of snow. The
youngsters are pulling each other about on sleighs and
giving us a snowball on the sly.

It doesn't suit us, though, all this snow as we have to go out in it on stunts just the same. We had a terrible day yesterday. Stan didn't start on his course as the roads were in too bad a condition.

Stan's mother and family seem to have taken to us alright. I wouldn't be surprised if he did visit you on his leave. I've an idea he will, love.

The fuel situation is a bit rough, pidge. We can't get anything for the stove where we sleep, but the old lady invites us into the kitchen when we are about. We came in yesterday cold and wet and she wasn't two minutes in getting some steaming hot coffee for us. There's no mistake about it, she is good to us.

Yes, darling. I well remember my last seven days leave. We had got something to look forward to every three months, hadn't we? Besides two 48 hrs or a 96 hr in between. What a lot has happened since then, darling. Still, we must think ourselves lucky in many ways. I did manage to get home for Dorothy's first birthday. I'm afraid it won't be so this time, darling, however I'll be satisfied if the Lord spares me to be there for her third.

[To Nan from Stan Middleton]

X Coy
9 January

Yes, George and I have founded a firm friendship. It is the greatest thing of all to have a friend whom you can trust and rely upon, especially during the times we have gone and are going through. During the last year we had some rather bad times. I don't wish to relate them, it is a subject I never mention to Mother. Our dear ones at home have enough to worry about without getting extra worry.

Am I getting excited about my leave? I should say I am. Mother says you would like me to pay you a visit. Well, I won't make any promises, Mrs Scragg, although I would very much like to meet you. If at anytime you could spare the time to spend a few days in Yorkshire, Mother would be very pleased. Anyhow, that's a subject you and Mother will decide upon.

[From George]

X Coy
14 January

I often wonder if Dorothy remembers me, love. I don't
expect she does, really, at that age. I can see her getting
round her Dad easy enough when I come home. I do miss
her, bless her little heart. Life would be very empty for us
both without her, wouldn't it? She soon picks things up.
Fancy her trying to break nuts with her little shoe. I think
she must take after you, pidge, I know how you like them.
I do like to hear of her little sayings and doings. I'd never
tire of reading them.

Well, darling, the news is pretty good today. Old
Jerry is being rolled back again and the Russians are going
well. I hope it won't last much longer, but he's doing his
best to hang on. What his idea is I don't know, for his
doom is sealed. Sooner or later he's bound to crack up.

X Coy
21 January

It's great to listen to the news these days. The Russians are
smashing through all German resistance. I honestly think
three to six months will see it over, darling. He's hard
pressed on all sides now, isn't he?

A flying bomb chugged over last night. We could see
it quite plain. The guns opened up at it, but failed to bring
it down, although they have done very well round here,
pidge.

We all went for a look round one of the gun sites. It
reminded me of the good old searchlights days, darling. I
grumbled then, but honestly I wasn't in the army
compared to what I've been through since leaving them.
Still, I'll have no regret if I can get through safely and be
spared to come home to you and our little Dorothy.

She must be very interesting now, love, and so
knowing. Fancy her saying 'Daddy's letters' and 'Stan's
letters'.

X Coy
24 January

We had another good fall of snow during the night and it's
been freezing hard all day. I don't think I've been so cold as
I was today. We were out on the tanks doing small
schemes. I was very pleased to get back to the billets and a
fire.

    The woman put us out a plate of soup each, which
was very welcome. She certainly does her best for us. We
haven't got any coal for our stove, so all of us get round
the one in the kitchen at night and either make a jug of
coffee or cocoa. One night it's Stan's turn and another
mine. It's nice to have a drink before turning in as supper is
early, ½ past 6.

    We missed the six o'clock news tonight as the electric
didn't come through till a quarter past, but we shall be able
to get the nine. The people heard the news in Belgian and
said that the Russians were less than 100 miles from Berlin.

X Coy
30 January

Darling, it's very cold out here. The people here were
telling us that a young baby was frozen to death in a
neighbouring village the other night in bed. It's hard to
believe, but it appears to be true.

    I'm sorry to hear that your mother is so short of coal.
It must be very worrying for them. It's nice to be able to
help them out a bit, but you can't run short yourselves
with having the two kiddies to think about, can you? I can
hear you and Mary miss your bedmates this cold weather,
love, but no more than we miss you, I bet. Do you take
up the hot water bottles, love? Still, they are a poor
substitute, aren't they, darling?

    The woman here is busy baking cakes tonight. They
are very good, love, despite the fact they can't get the right
amount of ingredients to make them.

At the beginning of February 1945, George and his friends
were moved from their happy billet with the Laermans

family in Autgaerden village, as preparations began for the last battle of X Company with the 1st Welsh Guards. In the event, all their training with tanks was hardly needed, for the Germans blew up the Roer dams, causing floods which made the armoured columns grind to a halt. 'Operation Veritable', the battle for the Rhineland, became for the most part a muddy and bloody slugging match between infantry and artillery, with the bogged-down tanks toiling in their wake as best they could.

X Coy
1 February

Well, pidge, we've moved out of the village, worse luck, to some other billets not a great distance away. It's a large house, dozens of rooms in it, but it's not half so comfortable as where we were before. No fires, lights or water and it's a bit hard lying on the floor after having plenty of straw for a bed. However, we could be a lot worse off, couldn't we?

The old lady at the house cried when we told her we had to leave. She was really upset. She gave us the address and told us to write to her and call if we ever had the chance or go for a holiday after the war. She made us a big tin of cakes and gave us a tin of sugar each. You can't forget those kind of people, can you?

I'm pleased to say the thaw has set in here, love, hardly any snow to be seen now. But oh, the mud. It's over boot tops outside. We've had a do at getting rid of some of it, but didn't meet with much success. The more you move the more seems to come. You must have had it very cold, love, to freeze your hot water bottle.

Dearest, it will soon be six years since that great day when we were joined together. We haven't spent much of it together, have we, darling? But I hope it won't be long before we are united once again, never to be parted. It was the happiest day of my life, dearest, although there has been some happy ones since.

X Coy
12 February

This is the fourth billet we've had since leaving the village, pidge. I'm browned off with packing and travelling from place to place, but I expect it would be worse if we were at the front.

The weather is rotten, raining practically all the time, although it snowed heavy last night and it was a white world this morning.

Well, love, I wasn't surprised to hear of Helen – at all. There's lots of things like that happens to girls like that in any of the branches of the women's services. But, as you say, it's a big let down for her family. Still, her father has been a 'character' in his day, hasn't he? [Phrased in these terms, this could refer only to an illegitimate pregnancy. Although George obviously believes in the then current double standard of sexual morality, that there are 'girls like that' and good girls, his comparison of the behaviour of father and daughter shows that his views are not, perhaps, as rigid as those of many of his generation.]

X Coy
14 February

I'm so sorry about the parcel, love. I think it's one of the meanest tricks anyone can stoop to, and to think it's someone who is dug away in a comfortable job while we are in the thick of it makes it worse. I don't like wishing harm to anyone, but to do a thing like that is out of all reason, isn't it?

Still, no good comes of thefts like those.

Perhaps it's with having to write the contents on them that takes their eye. However, love, I'll take your advice and send no more parcels.

It's not the cost of the things that I think of, it's the disappointment for you. I know how you were looking forward to it. And to think it's been done by your so-called *comrades*. Still, there's no more decency in some of them than there is in a pig. I'd just like to have him on his own for five minutes. He'd think twice about doing such a thing again, love.

[Never, in any of his letters, did George express such anger; not against the war which had robbed him of his young married life, not the army with its petty rules and manifold quirks and injustices, nor the enemy he had been trained to destroy.]

By the middle of February, X Company had moved up to play their part in the border battle. The company carried out the capture of the village of Hassum by 'artificial moonlight', a new system of flooding a target area with searchlights and flares, designed to aid night assaults and blind the defending troops. Although the village was taken without casualties, many of the Scots-Welsh soldiers were injured during the next few days by the heavy artillery counter-attack poured into the area by the Germans. Guardsman Scragg spent his daughter's second birthday, 20 February, soaked with rain and caked with mud, sheltering from the barrage of shells. The soldiers remained in this area, carrying out patrols, until the beginning of March.

X Coy
19 February

It's terrible weather, foggy and raining most of the time. You can't dig a trench here, after it's a foot deep it fills up with water. What we want is a boat, I think. We are in a mess, I can tell you.

I thought about twelve months ago, darling, how I got home just in time for our Dorothy's first birthday party. Little did I think I should be going through this lot. Give her an extra big hug for me, love, and lots of birthday kisses. I only wish I was there to make them real ones.

Oh, love, thank them all for the contents of the parcel. They were very nice, but please don't send any more toffees. I felt as though I was robbing the kiddies when I was eating them. Besides we get some, pidge, so don't put any in again, will you?

X Coy
24 February

It's a grand day again, but it was raining heavy during the
night, so that meant bailing out the trench more often.

We are still doing well for food, love, ham, eggs,
chips and beans for dinner and there's six fowl to pluck for
teatime. There's no need for army food, only bread and
tea.

We've been for a look round the guns this morning
and saw them firing. They got a patrol of us out of a tight
corner the other day, our Dorothy's birthday it was, so I'll
always remember her second, love. It was like heaven to
get back to the old trench, even if it is half full of water.

I'm pleased Dorothy had plenty of birthday presents,
love. I'll see about having some of my money changed to
postal orders when we get out again and then I can send
her some for a savings certificate.

[To Nan from Minnie Middleton]

Staincross
25 February

Wasn't the person who tampered with the parcel a cad,
Mrs Scragg? To rob soldiers' parcels or parcels they send
home is nothing short of a crime in my estimation and it is
hard luck, our men fighting for dirty brutes to behave in
that manner. We were terribly sorry for you, Mrs Scragg
and for George too, having spent his money, for people to
steal a child's present. My husband said an electric battery
would be the ideal thing to attach to the fingers of such
people.

Stan mentions how everything is muddy and wet. It
does make us feel sorry when we are so comfortable. They
are moving on, according to the news, and if the weather
will be favourable it would help immensely.

You know we are longing to see Dorothy. She will be
at a very interesting age now. She will be a real pal to you
until Daddy is home and a comfort too.

PS Tuesday 26 February Hurrah, I have received a

letter this morning from your husband and Stan and they
are OK. That is grand. He says how very much they
appreciate each other's comradeship. It is lovely for us to
know, dear.

[From George]

X Coy
28 February

We are out of the trenches at last, love, billeted among
Jerry civvies. They are still in some of the houses. I
thought they would have cleared out when we came, but
no, they seem content to stay behind. They seem harmless
enough, but, of course, you can't afford to take risks.

We shan't be having such good food now, pidge, as
we don't 'knock off' the hens, pigs, etc., if the civvies are
still there. So we'll be on the old army stuff again, I
suppose. However, we had a good run while it lasted, love.

I honestly think this war will be over before I get my
leave. Stan won't be going next month even and will be
lucky to get away in April, so you can imagine how long
I've to wait. However, as long as we get through it alright
I don't mind so much about the leave. But, all the same,
I'd love to be home with you and our little treasure for a
spell, dearest.

In an envelope addressed to Nan, postmarked 5 March
1945, George sent two postcards of Autgaerden signed by
the Laermans family, and a newspaper clipping which read:

As the Allies advance over this prosperous farmland
they find increasing numbers of German civilians,
particularly older folk, staying in their homes.

In addition large quantities of foodstuffs are being
left behind, as well as herds of cattle, flocks of chickens
and pens full of pigs – instead of the scorched earth
being called for by Goebbels.

It is a question of leaving the livestock to starve
or eating it. Our frontline troops are having little
difficulty making a decision.

X Coy
4 March

I'm pleased to hear you can go for a nice walk again now, without being troubled with the pram, love. You would enjoy going across the mill meadows again after all that time.

So our Dorothy thinks I should be on all the trains that go by, love? What a day that will be when I'm on one again, but I'm afraid there will be a lot go through Armitage before mine comes, dearest. She seems very intelligent for her age, doesn't she? I bet you have many a laugh at her sayings, pidge.

Between 6 March and 10 March, X company were again in action, fighting for high ground east of the Rhine and driving towards the Rheinberg–Xanten railway. They took the village of Bonninghardt, but their officer, Captain A. N. B. Ritchie, was wounded and in the heavy shelling tanks were bogged down and destroyed.

The British soldiers were being used as 'bait' to draw German resources away from the big thrust in the American section of the front. The flooding from the burst dams delayed the American attack and allowed the Germans to concentrate on the British. Division histories record that the Germans 'fought desperately for every house, cottage and shed and kept up a tremendous fire from their artillery'.

But by 7 March, the Americans had taken Cologne and the West bank of the Rhine to Coblenz.

[To George from Minnie Middleton]

Staincross
6 March

Our thoughts are very often of you and Stan and we do appreciate the bond of comradeship. Yes, friendship is a valuable possession and especially at this time. We feel like you about it, George, that it will be a lasting friendship, to continue long after the war is over.

Stan tells me in his recent letter that it will probably

be May before he gets his leave now. I can hardly express the disappointment it has meant to us. You see, we were all built up that it was to come in Feb. It is over a year since he had his leave. Nevertheless there is the looking forward that is helping us all and if the fighting can be finished we could bear the separation just a little longer from those of you who we love so dearly, to know that you were safe and well.

X Company in the Scots Guards, spring 1945, George is fourth from left on the second row from back; Nan kept this picture rolled up and kissed it so often that it is impossible to see him.

We were so sorry to hear how Dorothy's parcel had been pilfered. I won't state in my letter what I would like to give the one responsible. What ever are you lads fighting for but these? Here are two lines from that poem Monty quoted in our paper 'A kinder world – A cleaner breed.' We hope it can be so.

[To Nan]

X Coy
7 March

I'm alright, pidge, but I'm sorry I haven't been able to write before. However, you can understand how things are, love. We've been *busy* these past few days.

I've just had a little nap, Stan is down now. We haven't had much sleep for a day or two. It was a long day yesterday, up at four and on till about nine at night. We were absolutely done up.

The civvies decorate up the houses with anything white. As I look out from here there's sheets, etc., flying everywhere. It's time they packed the job up, don't you think, love?

X Coy
11 March

I think we shall soon be going out for a rest. It seems all quiet up to the Rhine now. The news is very good isn't it? The Yanks have soon made the other side. I think Jerry is fast crumbling now. Once the bulk of the armour gets over they will run rings around him.

I'm longing for the sunny days to come again, but the wettest, coldest days would be the sunniest if we were together again, darling.

After the Rhineland Battle, the Guards were pulled back to the Nijmegen area for rest and reorganisation. A farewell parade marked the parting of the ways for the 1st Welsh and X Company, who joined the 2nd Battalion of their own

189

regiment, the Scots Guards. But there was no room for them as a company, so the men were dispersed among other units.

X Coy
13 March

Well, dearest, I've got something extra special in the way of news. All being well, I shall be with you all again before the month is out. I don't know the exact date at the moment, darling, but I'll let you know as soon as I get it. Stan goes on the 21st, I believe, so we should both be over during some part of the leave.

I can hardly believe it's true, darling, but it is and that's the main point.

We are back in the same village as when we were in the old barn, but we've got into a school this time, love. I don't know how long we shall be here. I hope long enough to get my leave before anything else big comes off, love. I'm keeping my fingers crossed, darling.

So our Dorothy expects me to bring her some toffees, does she, pidge? If we were in Belgium it would be easy enough, but here there's nothing. However, we'll make the very best of it and hope it won't be long before we are together for always.

Chin up, keep smiling, darling. Give our little treasure a big hug and lots of x x x x for me. It won't be long before they are real ones, love. Don't forget to air the old suit, darling.

X Coy
17 March

Well, pidge, I've been told the date I start on leave, a little later than I thought, April the fourth. However, the time will soon pass, won't it, love? Stan went yesterday, he said he might pay you a visit, but it's uncertain.

The General inspected us this morning and we all had our photographs taken. I hope it turns out OK and in time for the 4th, love.

It's a grand day. I expect the kiddies are out enjoying

David Yardley and Dorothy, early 1945.

the sunshine, either playing in the garden or out walking. We'll be able to go some nice walks when I come home now that Dorothy's older. I've been wondering what she will be like with me. I bet she will think it strange for a day or two.

Yes, love, I think a few more months should see it over, but we want a few more crossings over the Rhine yet. The weather should soon be favourable for it, and then for the knock-out.

Scots Guards
B Coy 40 RHU
101 RFT Group
BLA
19 March

No doubt you will be surprised at the address, but it's all for the best. Not much chance of anything happening before I've had my leave now, darling.

There's been a lot happening these last few days. I can't tell you all, but most of us who are due for leave have come here. It seems strange to us, a bed each with a mattress. It's a long time since we had the pleasure.

There's a huge NAAFI, one of the best I've seen, and pictures every night. It seems too good to be true, but it's there alright. We've been up for a medical inspection and nearly all of us had a 'noc'. I thought I should have been clear, but no, I had to have a Typhus.

Well, darling, the weather is grand. I do hope it's like this when I'm on leave so that we can all get out, love. It seems strange to be talking of leave, doesn't it, love? I can hardly realise it, you know, after all this time. I expect it will be some time before I hear from you. The mail will be all over the show, I suppose.

The 'Blighty Station' is close by. I expect Stan will be reporting back here when he comes back. I think our 'partnership' will be broken up now. We put our names down to stay together, but somehow I don't think we shall be. It will seem strange without him after all this time. We've always been together through thick and thin, even on night patrols etc.

B Coy
20 March

We've been out training with some of the lads who haven't tasted battle yet and it was real hot in the sun.

I had a walk out tonight, just looking round the shops. There's plenty to buy, with plenty of money as usual, silk stockings, hankies, fountain pens, scent, hair clips and lots of toffees, so I'll be alright for bringing a few things home now, love.

The leave roster is up on the notice board. I start on the 3rd. Of course, it's subject to alteration, but if there is any, I think it will bring me forward. I expect Stan is enjoying his leave. It's all too short, isn't it? But still, it's very welcome.

[From Minnie Middleton]

Staincross
4 April

Dear Mrs Scragg
There is no need for me to ask how you are feeling just now because you will be just about overcome with excitement and thrilled beyond words at looking forward to your dear husband getting home, if he hasn't already arrived.

Dorothy had her cut
April 25ᵗʰ 1944

We hope you will have the happiest seven days that is possible to have. It is a time that has been long looked and waited for, I know, and if you look at him every minute that you have him, it won't be one moment too much, bless him.

I think I so stared at Stan during the time I had the chance that I could scarcely keep back the emotion. You see, he went amongst his friends and everyone wanted to see him so that he didn't have a great deal of time in the home.

I'll just confide this to you. He came in one night at 12 pm and said, 'Make me a cup of tea, please, Mum.' Well, he got down in a chair and fell fast asleep before the tea was handy. I couldn't waken him, so I got comfortable in a chair and just sat looking at him until three in the morning. But I enjoyed every minute of it. It was grand. I had often tried to picture him in the chair while he was over there in the fighting and my chance came and, believe me, I wouldn't have missed it for all the world.

*George and Nan had this
family portrait taken during his
final leave in April 1945, a
copy of which was in Nan's
last letter – once again Nan has
kissed George's face away.*

Chapter Twelve

'Thanks for the Memory'

For seven spring days in April, George Scragg became again what, in his heart, he had always been; a family man, absorbed in the delight of his wife and child. Simple pleasures, like a walk picking daisies in the meadows by the river with Nan and Dorothy or a visit to the cinema, a pint at the pub or a chat to family and friends – these were memories to hoard like a miser, a talisman of normality to buffer him for his return to the fighting.

At the end of his leave, as she waved him goodbye, Nan, in whom simple religion and traditional country superstitions co-existed in apparent harmony, spoke to her twin sister Mary Yardley.

'As he walked away from us down the hill, she turned to me and said, "That's it. I shan't see him again." I don't know what made her say it. We were all worried, because we knew the fighting was very hot, but Nan just had that sudden feeling that she knew he would not come back.'

On 18 and 19 April the Scots-Welsh group attacked Visselhovede, where their headquarters had to be rescued by a tank group after being surrounded by German Marines. A bitter battle for the town of Rotenburg ended with the capture of 200 German prisoners.

Belgium
15 April

Well, darling, I thought I'd write and let you know that
I've crossed safely and that I'm alright, love. We sailed
yesterday, but for some reason they turned back after nine
miles, so we had another night in old England. It was a bit
galling to think I might have had an extra day with you
and our little treasure, darling.

Dearest, I feel rather unsettled after such a lovely
week, but I suppose I shall have to get accustomed to it for
a little while longer. I'm sure it was the happiest seven
days leave we have spent together and I'm looking
forward to years of the same happiness, darling.

It did upset me to leave you both, dearest. No-one
knows what it's like, do they, who haven't gone through
it? But never mind, darling, it makes the bonds of love so
much stronger, doesn't it, love? And more so when
you've got a little one to love.

Well, dearest, there was one thing I forgot and I
missed it before I got to Lichfield and that was the photo of
the three of us. So when I've got settled again will you
send it, love? I don't know how I forgot it as I treasure it so
much, darling.

Darling, this time last week we were enjoying
ourselves at the pictures. How I wish we were doing the
same tonight. However, we must hope and pray that it
won't be long before we are all enjoying the happiness that
has been barred to us for so long. I'm sure it can't be for
much longer, darling.

So, for now, chin up and keep smiling, darling. Don't
worry too much. I'll take care to the best of my ability.
Tell Dorothy it won't be long before her Daddy is home
again with his little Dotto.

V Coy
17 April

We arrived back to V Coy last night after 24 hours
continuous travelling. What a journey it was, but our
lovely week together was worth it all, dearest.

Did Dorothy go up the Common lanes for a walk?

She gets a card, doesn't she, love? By the way, pidge, send me one or two 'dicky daisies' she's picked herself, will you? I should like to have them, love. I can't give you an address as we are probably moving again today, but I'll let you know it as soon as possible.

It's a grand day, but, oh, what a difference to last week. I've been thinking about it all the time. It was great, wasn't it, darling? I hope there's years of it ahead for us, love.

I expect I shall be seeing Stan sometime during the next few days. I hope I get with him, but they can stick me just where they like, it's all the same to me, love.

I'll take care of myself to the best of my ability, so don't worry too much, dearest. Give our little treasure a big hug and lots of x x x x for me, love. I hope it won't be long before they are real ones again. Don't forget the photos, love, as soon as I get settled, will you? Take care of yourself and Dorothy, and don't worry, darling. I put my trust in the One above.

[To Nan from Minnie Middleton]

Staincross
18 April

I have thought of you very much since George returned to BLA.

You will be feeling not so good I am sure because I know what the going back means to us all. But try and keep cheerful and well and look forward to the end of the war being not far hence. We have hoped now for such a long time that it is hard to bear and the suspense seems sometimes to get too much, doesn't it, dear?

I think Stan looks a little older now than I expected to find him but of course, it is the conditions. We really can't wonder, can we? Oh, but wasn't it grand to see them? It was just lovely. When Stan peeped round the door you can guess my feelings and I am certain of yours when George walked in at your home.

[From George]

Right Flank Coy
2nd Batt Scots Guards
23 April

We are just having a little rest after a stiff week of it. It's a treat to relax, I can tell, you, love. The weather is typical of April. These showers soon wet you through, then out comes the sun and dries you up again.

I shall be very pleased when I begin to get your letters again, darling. It's rotten to have no mail, still, they will soon begin to arrive, I hope.

I did have some letters the other day, but, of course, they were all written before I went on leave, so they wasn't so interesting, love.

I see Stan pretty often. He's alright and I think he is taking some stripes, according to what he told me this morning. I'm just getting to know the fellows here, now, but I didn't get much chance before. I joined one night and we were away the next morning.

According to the papers it's 'All over bar the shouting', but, believe me, it's hard going yet. I shouldn't like to say when it will be over. He's beat, he knows that, but he will still fight on.

Give our Dorothy a big hug and lots of kisses for me. Tell her I'll go picking daisies and dandies with her again some day. Chin up, keep smiling. I'll write whenever possible, dearest.

As the invading troops penetrated deeper into the heart of Germany, they encountered a lost army of prisoners of war and forced labour workers. Some of them had been simply dumped by the retreating Germans and left to wander the roads in pathetic bands, half-starved, ragged and bewildered in an alien country. The joy of freeing Allied servicemen from captivity was soured by bitterness and anger as, one by one, the concentration camps revealed the true horror of which human beings were capable.

Right Flank Coy
24 April

My dearest Nan

Well, darling, just a few lines to let you know I'm alright and hope you are all well at home, love. It's a lovely morning, hardly a cloud in the sky, and the sun is real warm.

I went to the baths yesterday afternoon. It's grand to get the dirt off yourself. I met Jock Williamson there, the chap who went back to Blighty last Sept with a poisoned finger. I never thought I should see him out this way again. I looked out for Toby when I was there and made enquiries too, but I got nowhere.

Well, dearest, with not hearing from you, I hardly know what to write about, but I expect just a few lines are welcome.

There's lots of nationalities about here, French, Poles, Russians. They seem delighted to be freed. Some look well enough, but others seem in a bad way. There are scenes you can't forget.

Well, pidge, I expect our Dorothy still goes over the meadows picking her flowers. I picture her many times, stooping there with her daisies. I realise, more so now after spending such a lovely week with you, what we are missing by being parted.

However, darling, let's hope and pray that we shall soon be together again with no more partings. Surely this can't go on much longer now without some decision being reached.

Well, love, I haven't got a lot more news, so will close now,

From your everloving husband.
xxx George xxxx

Cheerio, darling, and may God Bless you and keep you both safe always. Give our little treasure a big hug and lots of xxx for me. Chin up, keep smiling, love. Give my love to all at home.

That was to be the last letter George Scragg wrote to his wife. A new attack was ordered, with two objectives – to support the major assault on Bremen and to liberate the nearby prisoner-of-war camp at Westertimke, which held 8,000 British, Commonwealth and Allied captives.

A few months later, Stan Middleton told Nan in a letter that he had spoken to George, who was now in a different platoon, the night before the attack, and that George seemed to feel that he would not survive. Forty years later, Stan could not recall the words, but he remembered the instinct as one that was recognised among soldiers.

'We never talked about the possibility of dying, but it was true that some people got the feeling that they weren't going to come through it. It never happened to me, no matter how dangerous a situation was. But we knew, even if they didn't say it in words, that it was something that was just there for some people.'

At first light on the morning of 26 April, the Scots-Welsh group passed through the newly-taken small town of Zeven. A mile outside the town, they hit a road block and German self-propelled guns opened up a devastating fire from woods on either side.

Stan, whose platoon was nearby, remembered, 'George was killed instantly. I identified him.' He paused, then added in a low voice, 'He was almost unrecognisable.'

During the battle, senior officers refused the offer of a ten-hour truce to allow the safe handover of the Wester-timke prisoners because they believed it was a ploy to cover the withdrawl of German Panzer troops. The camp was finally taken on the morning of 28 April.

A letter to his wife after the battle from Lieut.-Col. H. N. Clowes, commanding the 2nd Battalion Scots Guards, showed that the two-day fight for Westertimke had cost 75 casualties.

He wrote: 'We had the most appalling shelling that anyone out here has ever known. It simply never stopped from dawn to dusk and 90 per cent of our casualties were from it . . . It was worthwhile enduring during the shelling to see the joy of those liberated men. They were all in terrific form and had been treated very well indeed, especially just lately.'

The letter ends, with the relief of the survivor. 'These

last two days have been very hectic and I hope never again to experience such intense shelling. It is wonderful what a bottle of champagne will do in the evening!'

On 30 April Adolf Hitler committed suicide as his Berlin bunker shook to the onslaught of the advancing Russians. By 8 am on 5 May, when a ceasefire had been agreed, the tally of casualties in the Guards Armoured Division since George Scragg had rejoined the fighting on 16 April was 116 killed, 483 wounded and 66 missing.

Stan Middleton was reluctant to describe the feelings of a soldier who sees a friend and comrade die. 'You don't have time to think much about it. You can't let yourself think too much. You have to go on and finish the job.'

Later, when the conversation turned to anger and aggression, he said, 'You see a friend killed and that might decide whether the next enemy you see becomes a prisoner or a corpse. That sounds callous, but it's true. War brings out the worst side of human nature.'

Stan's wife, Renee, suggested, 'And the best side, too.' Stan remained silent.

On the night of 30 April 1945, Nan parcelled up the photographs that George had forgotten, and slipped in a note telling him about washday and the spring cleaning she and Mary had been doing.

'I hope you will get the photos alright,' she wrote. 'I'll bet you have missed them, for it's nice to have a look at us both sometimes, isn't it? It sort of makes you feel nearer to us.

'Mary is writing to Ted as well. We are both nearly asleep over our letters. I shall be glad to roll into bed tonight. I expect you've missed your bedmate, love, since you went back, but, never mind, if all's well and you are spared to come through this last bit safely, we shall have a lot to make up for.'

The package was returned to her by the regimental records office in September. It had arrived too late.

By the end of April, the foreboding which Nan had expressed to her sister as George left her had deepened. One day she confided it to a friend as they walked home from Church. The friend tried to reassure her. 'No news is good news. You'll hear from him soon. He's just busy.'

Nan's letter to George which arrived too late; she kept it exactly as it was returned to her.

On 7 May, as a European ceasefire became general, three letters were posted to Nan Scragg, care of the Swan Inn, although for more than a year she and Dorothy had been sharing the Yardleys' cottage further up the village's main street.

One, from Yorkshire, brought Minnie Middleton innocently into the irony and drama that was about to explode into the lives of the two families in Brereton and Armitage.

Staincross
7 May

I had a letter from George dated April 24. He is not in the same platoon as Stan now, he tells me, but in the same Coy and would be able to see him often. But in two letters from Stan now he says how he misses George very much now that he hasn't him to talk to, but he doesn't give the reason. So I wonder if they have got separated again because as soon as they get used to their pals the army has a habit of moving them. That is a fault Stan did grumble about.

But the news is giving us great hopes now and the next we are longing to hear is that hostilities have ceased. I dare say George will get home to you much sooner than Stan because of his having joined the regulars. You see, he has 4 years to serve before he is on reserve. But if the fighting can be finished I shan't worry perhaps like if it was still continuing. Still there are the Japs to get down.

Well, dear, I hope you will be coming to visit us before long because George said in his letter that you would all pay us a visit after the war and we shall look forward to it. We are longing to see Dorothy, bless her.

The second, an oblong buff envelope, was waiting for Nan at the Swan Inn on 8 May, with half the world preparing for the Victory in Europe celebrations.

The envelope contained Army Form B104-82B. Nan Scragg's 'obedient servant', the colonel in charge of the Scots Guards record office, Buckingham Gate, London, fulfilled his painful duty to inform her that her husband had been killed in action eleven days before in Germany and expressed the sympathy and regret of the Army Council at the soldier's death in his country's service.

'She gave a terrible scream,' Nan's sister Mary said. 'She just went completely to pieces.'

While Nan's brother-in-law Jack Smith was despatched on his bicycle to take the news to Brereton, Nan remained that day at the Swan. Years afterwards, she described her feelings. 'Everyone was downstairs in the pub, celebrating the end of the war, drinking and singing, and I had lost my husband. I thought I was mad.'

The official notification of death.

203

A few days later, another letter, postmarked 7 May, arrived from George's unit commander, Major Digby Raeburn.

My dear Mrs Scragg

I am writing to offer you my deepest condolences on the death in action of your husband, Guardsman Scragg. He was killed instantaneously by a shell during our attack on a big wood just west of the German town of Zeven. He is buried near where he fell along with his officer who was killed just before him.

Owing to our fighting and movements since it has not yet been possible to visit his grave, but you may rest assured that it will be well cared for and visited as soon as our circumstances permit.

I hope it will afford you some measure of consolation to know that the attack in which your husband was killed led to the liberation of many thousands of British prisoners of war. He did not die in vain.

Please again accept my deepest condolences on your tragic loss.

It was to be one of the last such letters Digby Raeburn had to write during that campaign, his painstaking, neat hand-writing expressing the professional soldier's difficulty in explaining the hard price of his trade to outsiders.

Digby Raeburn was a year younger than George, a product of Winchester public school and Magdalene College, Cambridge. He went on to command not only the 2nd Battalion Scots Guards, the regiment and the brigade, but to become Chief of Staff to the Commander in Chief Allied Forces in Northern Europe, Chief Instructor at the Imperial Defence College and a Freeman of the City of London. By the time he retired, he was Major-General Sir Digby Raeburn and had completed eight years as Governor of the Tower of London and Keeper of the Jewel House.

The General did not remember George Scragg; he had been too recently transferred to his company at the time of George's death, but he remembered the battle.

'That may have been about the last letter of condolence I had to write. We were the leading company then, and for the rest of the battle other companies were in the lead and I don't think we had many casualties after that. One did one's best to give what consolation one could to the widow, or in most cases it was to the mother. You were restricted by security and, really, what could you say except he was a valued member of the team and he had done his duty?

'It never got easier. When you are fighting, you get inured, in a way, to casualties. You feel quite relieved when you hear someone has only been wounded. But you get more upset when it is someone you know better. It was more upsetting to me when I lost a valued section commander than a Guardsman I had hardly known.'

Adjusting to sudden, violent death is part of a soldier's job; his sanity depends on a kind of mental anaesthesia. 'You had to. If you didn't, where were you? You could never live with your friends or yourself again. There were a few people it was too much for, but not the majority. Really, you could say that the British Army is never an army that likes fighting, but when it has to, it does it and does it very well.'

Throughout May, letters of sympathy, their envelopes franked with the joy bells of victory, arrived for Nan. Villagers, friends, scattered relatives, awed by the dreadful symmetry of the tragedy in the midst of their own rejoicing, fumbled for words of comfort.

The letters told Nan that George was a hero, that he had given his life that others might live in peace in a better world. Baffled at the finality of the loss at the moment when safety was within grasp, they tried to persuade Nan that there was a sense and meaning to it, so that they, too, could believe.

Some of the condolences must have hurt Nan through the simple, jarring conjunction of their acknowledgement of a death and the knowledge of both the writer and the recipient that life, for others, was going on. For this reason, letters like the well-intentioned note from the village's Welcome Home Committee, formed to greet returning servicemen, would burn Nan like acid.

From Barnsley, with the realisation of the meaning of the words in her son's letter about missing his friend, came the instinctive response of Minnie Middleton: compassion and horror, overlaid with the need to be of practical help.

Staincross
14 May

My dear Mrs Scragg

The news of your dear husband's death came to us a shock. We cannot realise it, dear. Although Stan had remarked in his letter to us that he missed George very much now that he hadn't him to talk to, I never wanted to think that he hadn't him in life.

We are grieved beyond words and our heartfelt sympathy goes out to you, dear, and we trust you will be given the help you so much need to bear your tragic loss. We are sincerely sorry for you and your family and George's dear Mother. We did so hope for his safe return.

I have written Stan that you wish for him to let you have news of George's burial and I am sure he will give you the comfort you so much need by doing all that he possibly can. If he can visit George's grave for you I know he will give you consolation by doing so. Stan and George were brothers in every respect. I like to think of the lovely and affectionate manner in which he wrote to me of you and little Dorothy in his letter of the 25th April. Bless her, she made her Daddy so happy.

If when you are feeling a little better, dear, you would care to have a stay with us we would do our best to make you comfortable. I remember you in my prayers, dear. Goodnight and God Bless you. Our love to you and Dorothy.

Yours in sympathy
M & A & Alice Middleton

And from the newly-promoted Stan Middleton, Nan received the painful attempt by a survivor to console the widow of his best friend.

Right Flank Coy
18 May

Dear Mrs Scragg
This is my first real opportunity to write you this letter. We have been on the move all the time for the last fortnight and we are off again tomorrow.

should be free from petty pilfering and destruction. I trust I shall hear no more complaints. One hesitates to call in the Police to help protect Church property; it should be considered too sacred to need such protection, and I hope I shall not be driven to take this course.

Roll of Honour. One addition had to be made to this just after the Victory in Europe celebrations, for news came through that George Scragg had lost his life while rescuing prisoners in Germany nine days prior to the German capitulation. It is sad that after serving so long he should be killed just at the very end and our sympathy and prayers go out to his widow and infant daughter, as well as to his many relatives. A goodly number of his relatives and friends attended the Requiem said for him on May 15th. May he rest in peace! His death brings our Roll of Honour up to eight to the end of the fighting in Europe, and this is mercifully small when compared with the last war, which did not last so long and when we remember that our list of those serving has reached over 260. We have much to thank God for. Also I hear

George is remembered in the parish magazine.

Please forgive me, Mrs Scragg, if I re-open the newly made wound in your heart. I do wish you to know how deeply grieved I am with George being killed. He was my friend – the best. At times, I just can't realise he isn't with me any more. Since last September we have been inseparable – slept together, ate together, and fought side by side.

Please accept my own heart-felt sympathy Mrs Scragg. The rest of the lads who George and I used to associate with also wish to be remembered to you.

Yours sincerely
Stanley

Nan kept George's wallet as it was when he died; amongst its contents were photographs of Nan, Mary and David Yardley, some cigarette cards, a prayer book and a decoration from his and Nan's wedding cake.

CERTIFICATE OF DEATH

CERTIFIED that according to a telegraphic communication received in this Department that *No 1659264 Guardsman George Scragg Scots Guards* ~~died at~~ *was killed in Action in Western Europe* on the *twenty-sixth* day of *April 1945*

Dated this *31st* day of *may* 1945

Signed *[signature]*

The War Office

No. D/185344 (Effects)

Effects Form 100T

D8984. M23177/5503. 10m. 12/44. M.T. 47/6.

George's death certificate.

Notification of the service of remembrance.

At the Service of Remembrance in St. Peters Church, Eaton Square, London, S.W.1, on Wednesday *May 16th 1945* at 12.15 p.m. *No 1659264 Gdsn. Scragg G. Scots Guards* will be remembered by name before God.

[signature]

Lieutenant-Colonel Commanding, Scots Guards.

Colonel,

P.T.O.

[To Nan from Minnie Middleton]

Staincross
5 June 1945

We have thought of you and little Dorothy more than we can express to you since the tragic news of George, dear. It is hard to realise it even yet. But we do hope, dear, that you are feeling a little better.

Stan wished to write to you but he says how it upsets him. George was his most loyal friend. I wrote him to ask him to carry out your wish but they had moved and were still on the move at the time and he was sorry not to be able. I have had a letter from him today and he is now back at Zeven and he has been able to get a camera and he is asking permission to visit the grave and take a photograph for you. He will do whatever he can to give you the comfort of knowing where George is because he was to him a brother and comrade, one of the best.

Stan says now that he has time to sit and think of the action he himself went through he wonders however he came through it. His pal whom he trained with in England, Eddie, is in hospital, wounded for the second time.

Well, dear, I will let you have whatever news I can get from Stan but, you know, dear, they don't have much to say. They are trained that way. You see, Stan is a lad in age really and I understand how he feels.

A change would do you good, dear, and if you feel you could come to us with little Dorothy, bless her, we would welcome you.

PS Perhaps you would like me to come to see you, dear. I would be only too pleased if it would be any comfort to you.

[Mrs Middleton visited Nan in the summer of 1945 and spent many hours talking to her and comforting her and George's mother. Nan's family were very impressed by her kindness and practical good sense.]

The details of where George was buried.

[To Nan from Stan Middleton]

Right Flank Coy
21 June

Dear Mrs Scragg
Some time ago I wrote you a letter expressing my heartfelt
sympathy at your loss of George.

From letters I have received from Mother, you cannot
have received my letter.

You wished me to try and find George's grave if at all
possible. We went to Zeven for a three week stay and I
spent hours looking for the grave but couldn't find it.

The day before we moved away from Zeven to our
new area, Cologne, I spent all the morning looking again.
This time I did find the grave. He is buried on the edge of a
wood with the branches of the trees overhanging the
grave. The civilians in a nearby house look after the grave
very well. It has white stones all round the edges and
flowers planted on top.

The enclosed flower is one I took off the grave to send
you and I know you will treasure it Mrs Scragg.

I have taken a photo of the grave with a camera I
borrowed off a friend – he was a friend of George too.
There are about another 20 films to take yet before the
spool is finished. But as soon as it is done and we can get
them developed I will let you have the photo straight
away.

If there is anything more, or anything you would like
me to tell you Mrs Scragg, please let me know, will you?
Yours sincerely
Stanley

Right Flank Coy
3 August

Dear Mrs Scragg
You may be thinking it is taking me a long time to reply to
your letter. I have been away on a fortnight's course in
Brussels and your letter has been chasing me about, till it
has finally caught up with me.

I quite understand the reason why you didn't reply to

my letter immediately, Mrs Scragg. I know how ill you would be feeling.

I'm very sorry, Mrs Scragg, but I shan't be able to give you a photo of George's grave. My pal sent the spool to be developed and not one of the 36 films on the spool came out. We are very annoyed at the matter because we did want you to have the photo.

Do I think George knew he wouldn't always come out safely? Well, during all the time I was with George, we had never talked about that subject until this particular evening before going up the line. I don't know what made George say those few words, unless he had some inner feeling that made him say them. As we were lined up for the attack, I saw George and had a few words with him. You wish to know how he was killed! Well, Mrs Scragg, I had been hoping you wouldn't ask me that question. Even though you are my best friend's wife, I won't tell you, Mrs Scragg.

I knew George and understood him, even though he didn't say, he wouldn't have me tell you. If only he could speak to me I know he would say, don't tell my wife. Please forgive me, Mrs Scragg, I'm only refusing for George.

Mrs Middleton continued to write to Nan and Dorothy for many years after the war, letters of warmth and genuine concern. She also befriended the Belgian family in whose home Stan and George were billeted, visiting them to thank them for their kindness. The two families still remain friends, spending holidays with each other.

Dorothy with her father's service medals.

'QUE SERA, SERA'

The demobilising armies discharged their recruits, who returned home to a post-war world of change and changing values. The former Allies concealed their mutual distrust scarcely long enough to exact a joint vengeance at the Nuremberg war crimes trials.

'I was obeying orders,' the defendants pleaded, turning the discipline which is a soldier's security into a defence for the indefensible. And, like a stone worn away by a drip of water, that discipline crumbled in the eyes of the generation growing up in the time the soldiers had bought for them.

'I did as I was told. I wasn't paid to think,' the veterans protested.

'Ah,' replied the arrogant young, 'But what if . . . ?'

And men who had sacrificed for those years the right to question, for whom there had been no 'what if . . . ?', looked at the new world and wondered, 'Is this what I fought for?' For the world paid lip-service to the war years, with memorials and remembrance parades, with films and books which trivialised war into spectacle and adventure.

Altered themselves by an experience incomprehensible to those who had not shared it, and often unwilling or unable to explain it, veterans took up the threads of a life which had evolved in its own fashion since they went away. The reality was often bruising to those who confronted it. Even the most faithful of the women had, of necessity, learned to cope alone and that independence, however

213

Nan with Dorothy and David Yardley just after the war.

Dorothy, John Smith and David Yardley on the beach.

unwanted and unlooked for, was hard to deny. Children who had grown with the idea that Daddy was a photograph on the mantelpiece were faced with a flesh-and-blood stranger who expected privileges, usurped the authority that had been exclusively their mother's, occupied her bed and demanded her time, love and attention. Some families crumpled under the strain. In Britain the post-war divorce rate soared to twice the 1930 figure.

Surrounded by a society determined to turn its back on the war or, at least, insisting that it should be remembered only in certain approved ways, Nan Scragg found herself, at the age of 27, almost literally a skeleton at the post-war festivities. She was an uncomfortable physical reminder of events that everyone was attempting to forget. The accepted wisdom of the time decreed that she would be brave, 'buck up' and carry on with her life for the sake of her daughter.

But the practicalities of motherhood had never been easy for Nan. Her sister Mary remembered, 'She had a bad time at the birth. She was small and Dorothy was a big baby – 9½ lbs, and Nan had never been very well or very strong. But she seemed afraid to take responsibility, that was the trouble. When Dorothy was a baby, she was afraid to bath her, and she was living with me, so I took over.'

With a large, loving family of intensely practical people around her, Nan occupied the role of the family romantic and dreamer. Her sisters and her mother were the experts – the needlewoman, the cooks, the jam-makers and the pickle-bottlers – while she was the pampered pretty one, the spoiled 'runt of the litter'.

Ironically, if this support had not been available, the sheer need to survive would have forced Nan out into the world. But even though her widow's pension was meagre, the fact that there was always someone on hand who, apparently, could provide what she needed, lessened the incentive to venture out. In the end, whether through a sense of 'loyalty' to George, which grew into a habit and a lifestyle through her well-developed sense of drama and romance, or from plain apathy, Nan drew the cocoon of her widowhood about her and retreated from the world, much to the dismay of her family.

'She had always depended on George,' said Mary, 'and she was never any good without him. She never did cope; I coped for her and Ted came out of the Army a year later and took over. George was everything to her and that was it. She just lost confidence in herself. She could have married again. But she never looked at another man, never even thought about it, or if she did, I think she felt Granny Scragg, George's mother, wouldn't have liked it.'

Caught between love and guilt, the family were unable to influence her, and eventually they became equally bound in the tyranny of Nan's grief.

'Everything about George became sacred to her,' said Mary. 'His picture, which she still kissed every night, her wedding dress and veil, which she would never lend to anyone else, even though clothes were so short.'

Ted Yardley, who took up the reins as father, not only to his own son David, but to Dorothy as well, remembered they felt Nan could have tried harder, for Dorothy's sake, but she wouldn't, and in the end Mary became the mother to both of the children. 'Even years later, if something about soldiers came on television while she was with us, it had to be switched off, or she would leave the room.'

Dorothy and David playing in the sea at Rhyl.

Mary said, 'She made the rest of us feel so guilty. I felt as though I had everything – Ted and David and a home of my own – and she had nothing. Sometimes, if the rest of us criticised her, she said, "It's alright for you, you've got your husband." She was a caring mother, she looked after Dorothy's welfare and education, but she nagged. When Dorothy was older and came home from college, within two days she would be round at my house because her mother nagged so. The rest of the family felt that Nan's was a wasted life. If George had come home, they would have been happy because he would never have let her go to pieces. His death changed everything for our whole family.'

Nan on her only visit to George's grave, 1966.

For Dorothy, the problems of a family trying to adjust to normal life were reversed. She had to find a place for herself alongside an idealised and sanctified relationship that never faced the normal abrasive realities of married life. She had to live up to the expectations of a man she had never known, to play gooseberry to a ghost. In the 1960s, both she and her mother made the pilgrimage to visit George's grave, where Dorothy planted flowers and saw her father's name inscribed on the roll of honour.

Dorothy's memories and feelings provide the real, and continuing, epilogue to the story.

DOROTHY'S STORY

*Nan holding her
granddaughter Emma in 1967.*

Death, when particularly cruel or untimely, is rather like a
pebble being thrown into water – the nearer you are to the
stone, the stronger the ripples will affect you. The well-
meaning and genuinely sympathetic person will tell you
gently, 'Time is a great healer.' What else can they say? The
effectiveness of these comforting words depends entirely
upon the person to whom they are spoken.

For my mother and my father's mother – and to a
certain extent me – time only served to intensify their
misery and grief.

Strangely, I do not remember actually being told I
hadn't a father. Perhaps I never was, but I always knew
there was somebody missing. When his name was mentioned, I would say to myself, 'That's him. That's my dad
they're talking about.' Living as we did with Auntie Mary,
Uncle Ted and my cousin David, in their house, my uncle
became my 'father', my cousin my 'brother'. My mother
played no part in the running of a home which, painfully,
was not hers, and in which we were 'lodgers'.

They must have been difficult years for us all, after the
war. After the celebrations were over, and my mother had
survived the initial impact of the news she had been dread-
ing but was also expecting, family life had to get back to
normal. But many families, like ours, had never been
normal, had never had a chance to become established. It
wasn't considered suitable to bring a child up in a public
house, and the house my grandparents had promised to my
parents on their marriage was not yet vacant. That is why
we moved in with Auntie and Uncle.

Times were austere, and we were brought up to be
careful, to value things and to share. But we two children
were happy, apart from the usual sibling squabbles, and
oblivious to any of the problems which inevitably come
when two families live together – lack of space, of privacy,
and living in each other's pockets.

From a very early age, however, I do remember feeling
very insecure, and frightened of going to bed in the dark. I
wasn't allowed to have the landing light on (again, looking
back, I suppose my mother was conscious of using someone
else's electricity), and I used to lie awake, listening to the

comforting sound of human voices downstairs. It is true that a mother's anxiety transmits itself to her child, and this is exactly what was happening to me.

A pattern began to emerge, whereby Uncle went to work, at the local pottery, Auntie did all housework and cooking, at which she was expert, while my mother looked after us children. We enjoyed the long walks she took us on – as long as they weren't too long! – and would go in all weathers, walking round Longdon and the Ridwares, until our cheeks and noses were blue, and we breathed 'smoke'. We learned lots about nature, the changing seasons, the habitats of birds. In spring we spent afternoons by the canalside, collecting frogspawn, fishing for tiddlers, picking irisis, king cups and lady smocks; in summer we picnicked by the river, and were allowed to paddle or swim; towards autumn it was blackberry picking time – how we hated getting scratched, or stung by menacing wasps! She must have missed my father very much during these early days of widowhood.

Eventually – I suppose I was six, maybe seven – a little cottage in the village became vacant and my mother and I moved in. It was literally 'two-up, two-down', with a 'back kitchen' stuck on the end, and an outside flushless loo. It was cosy, but it was not what Mum wanted; it wasn't the house she had been promised, for which she and my father had bought furniture, made wool rugs, measured up for curtains. To me, the move was a great blow. I was being uprooted from 'home', and taken away from my 'brother' and my 'family'. The old order of things was lost, and it was as if my mother and I were being cast adrift in a sea too deep for both of us. It seemed that from now on, any major decisions were to be shared between grandparents, aunts and uncles, because although my mother was the person to whom I was directly answerable, she, in turn, relied on someone else, so my respect for her in that sense could never quite be complete.

I loved her because she was my mother, and I felt sorry for her. For the same reason I respected her and obeyed her. But as a person she was totally devastated, utterly destroyed by a blow from which she was never to recover. One thing remained intact – her strong faith. She often said that it was this which pulled her through and, as the whole extended family was church-going anyway, we were all helped to a

Nan in her sixties.

Dorothy at her father's grave in the early 1960s.

Dorothy sits at the piano for which Nan paid £100, with Emma [back], Joe and Amy. Her other daughter, Charlotte, is now married and living in the USA.

greater or lesser degree by religion.

One of the things which my father had requested, should he not come back, was to 'educate her if she's worth it'. Consequently I was under great pressure to do well at school. I always wanted to please my mother – to bring a smile to her face or a light to her eye, to 'make things better'. For the same reason I also wanted very much to follow in the footsteps of cousin David, always held up to me by my mother as a shining example of 'a child who is a credit to his parents'. When he passed the eleven-plus to go to the local Grammar School, I was terrified I would not do the same. The day I came home with the letter to say I'd passed remains one of my life's highest points – the gateway to success! I think my mother was so keen for me to do well for the sake of my father, to keep his memory alive, that she left out the little details in her haste for me to be as good as other children who *had* got a father. Although we both knew we loved each other, I felt I could never get too close, or be too intimate. Now I realise that there was a vacuum immediately surrounding her body *and* soul which, though I wanted to fill, I couldn't get close enough to do so. That space was meant for somebody else, and it remained empty for 36 long years of widowhood.

All the family lived close by, the furthest away being my father's family at a distance of two miles. Otherwise, in the same village lived my maternal grandparents, three great aunts, and seventeen assorted aunts, uncles and cousins. It gave me a cosy feeling like a human safety net when things weren't going too well at home. Nearest were Auntie Vi and Uncle Charlie. I could chat to them from our kitchen window when they were in their washhouse. Auntie used to come and visit Mum in the evenings when I'd gone to bed, to keep her company. Uncle Charlie would always come round in the night if it thundered and lightened, because Mum and I were afraid. He also chopped our sticks. He was a 'ganger' on the railway, and got old 'sleepers' free, to make into logs and sticks. He was also the village barber, and I used to like watching him attack his victims with those deadly steel clippers! He was jolly. Auntie Vi was straight-laced and didn't like him smoking his Woodbines in the house.

Up the garden path lived dear old Auntie Dolly and

Uncle Frank – she was mum's oldest sister, he was Auntie Vi's brother. He was church warden, and we always joked that he spent more time at church than at home. We cousins even rewrote the hymn, 'The Church's one foundation is dear old Uncle Frank' (instead of 'Jesus Christ our Lord'). For some years he played in a dance band every Saturday night as his pay as chauffeur/gardener to some retired ladies was less than ten shillings a week. Uncle Frank encouraged my early inclination towards music by having me practise on their piano until I 'proved' myself by passing my first music exam; then my mother spent my father's savings by making the long trip to Birmingham with Uncle Frank, to buy me my very own piano, a reconditioned walnut upright costing £100. I was seven then, and it is still in full use today.

Ted and Mary Yardley at their golden wedding celebration in February 1989.

Auntie Dolly was small and round, like a dumpling, and usually very jolly. They always welcomed me and cheered me up. They were simple people in the nicest sense of the word. Their house seemed to be a calling place for the whole village; it always seemed busy and alive. For everyone who called there was a welcome, a kind word, a sympathetic ear, a warm smile. My mother and I often had meals there. It seemed as though my mother needed to 'latch on' to someone for safety. They had no children of their own but they loved everyone else's. Every year they gave a party in the church hall for the Sunday school children and everyone went home with a prize. Uncle Frank was a keen gardener (he did ours too), and he knew all those clever rhymes about the weather. Auntie Dolly was very kind and sympathetic to my mother. I think she tried hard to play the role of big sister, and share some of her burdens. My other Aunties said that she 'spoiled' my mother and that 'she should make her stand on her own feet'. But it's hard to stand on your own feet when the ground has been cut from underneath them.

Stan Middleton.

Christmas seemed strange after we had left my cousin's. Father Christmas suddenly disappeared, as did the anticipation of opening presents on Christmas morning with someone my own age. It must have been at those times that Mum felt her loss most; it must have been so lonely, so joyless. There were to be many more occasions, occurring with dreadful relentlessness, when the absence of her beloved overshadowed what should have been the happiest of milestones, such as my first day at the 'little school' in the village and the medals I won in piano exams. 'How proud your Dad would have been,' she used to say. Even the ordinary events which many children share only served as poignant reminders that we were not a complete family to share those occasions – joining the Church Choir, passing the eleven-plus, being church organist, the Girl Guides, playing at Town Hall concerts, 'O' and 'A' levels, college in London, becoming a teacher, getting married and providing the joy of grandchildren. It seems incomprehensible, after reading my parents' letters telling of their great desire to have a child and their unspeakable joy when I was born, that occasionally my mother would exclaim vehemently, 'I wish I'd never had you!' At the time it used to upset me terribly and make me wish I was dead. I would run to my grandmother's house for comfort and reassurance that I *was* wanted, and she would take me in her arms and gently explain that Mother didn't mean it and that she 'doesn't always feel very well'. She, too, was apparently fulfilling a promise made to my father that she would look after us, should he not return.

My 'Granny Scragg' was equally devastated, but in a different way. My father had been her longed-for son, bearing him after two or three miscarriages eight years after having Mary, her first child, and at the age of 40. My mother remembered meeting her for the first time, invited for Sunday tea when she and my father were courting, and Granny Scragg, in a huge white pinafore from shoulder to floor 'filled the entire doorway'. She had been a fine figure of a woman. I only knew her as an old and gentle, but griefstricken lady, bravely smiling through an even-present veil of tears. I am told that after the news of my father's death she never again went out, except to Armitage to visit my mother and me, never again went to Church (it was as if God had taken her beloved son from her) and never again wore anything but grey or black. When I was old enough to travel alone I used to visit her nearly every Saturday; an added bonus being that Auntie Mary [her daughter] lived next door, with Uncle Les and cousin Dennis, and they were always great fun.

Grandad Scragg reminded me of the ogre in *Jack and the Beanstalk* – big, dark and very strict. Underneath, though, his heart was soft, and I'm sure that he, too, grieved his loss as much as his wife did.

Although the pervasive feeling of tragedy touched all members of our large family, there were many, many happy times, leaving me memories which I shall always treasure. Wonderful holidays at Rhyl with Auntie Dolly and Uncle Frank, aunts, uncles, cousins (but rarely my mother); haymaking at my Aunt Nora's smallholding, in the long, hot summer holidays, with bird nesting, canal fishing, country rambles, milking cows; family gatherings for Christmas dinner at Auntie Dolly's, with as many as twenty relatives sitting like sardines around the table; holidays with Auntie Mary and Uncle Les to Llandudno and New Brighton; another relative's farm in Shropshire, where we picked fresh mushrooms in dew-drenched fields at dawn.

But anniversaries were always sad. It was with a mixture of pride and sorrow that we would put flowers on the War Memorial on 26 April (the morning he was killed), on 1 September (his birthday), 11 November (Remembrance Day) and a wreath at Christmas.

My mother actually looked forward to the day she would be reunited with him. Death held no dread for her. She died very quickly from a stroke brought on by severe diabetes, diagnosed too late to be checked.

I could not believe it, and shall never get over it.

Mum's everlasting wish was to be attired in her wedding dress, cremated, and her ashes laid in my father's grave in Germany. To this latter, the Imperial War Graves Commission graciously consented, and on 2 September 1981, a day after his birthday, after a brief simple ceremony at the graveside, my mother's ashes were gently put into their last resting place. The words on his gravestone, which my mother and I had had to choose years ago, spoke out: 'The souls of the righteous are in the hands of God'. Another chapter of my life was over.

POSTSCRIPT

George and Nan lie together in the military cemetary at Becklingen, near Bremen. For them, the last verse of George's favourite song, 'Danny Boy', has become a poignant fact.

> And when you come, and all the roses dying,
> If I am dead, as dead I well may be,
> Then come and find the place where I am lying,
> And kneel and say an Ave just for me.
> And I shall hear, though soft you tread above me.
> And so my grave will warmer, sweeter, be.
> And I shall hear you whisper that you love me.
> And I shall sleep in peace until you come to me.

In September 1981, following Nan's death, Dorothy buried her mother's ashes in George's grave, accompanied by Nan's grandchildren Amy, Joe and Charlotte.

ACKNOWLEDGEMENTS

Regimental records of the Scots Guards
The Imperial War Museum
Staffordshire county archives
Lichfield Mercury
Staffordshire Advertiser
The Scots Guards, 1919–55, David Hervey Erskine, Clowes
Corps Commander, Brian Horrocks, Sidgwick & Jackson
The World War II Fact Book, Christy Campbell, Futura
Encyclopaedia of World War II, general editor John Keegan,
    W H Smith
Now the War Is Over, by Paul Addison, Cape-BBC
The Battle for Normandy, by Eversley Belfield and
    H Essame, Pan
Six Armies in Normandy, by John Keegan, Penguin
Battle of the Ruhr Pocket, by Charles Whiting, Ballantine
The Battle of the Bulge, by Charles B MacDonald, Guild
Siegfried, The Nazis' Last Stand, by Charles Whiting,
    Granada
Soldiers, A History of Men in Battle, by John Keegan and
    Richard Holmes, Guild
Britain Under Fire, The Bombing of Britain's Cities 1940–45,
    by Charles Whiting, Guild
*'44, In Combat on the Western Front from Normandy to the
    Ardennes*, by Charles Whiting, Century

The help, advice, support and enthusiasm of many people
made this book possible; any omissions from this list are
due to lapse of memory, not lack of gratitude.

   To Maurice Blisson and Phil White, for love and
understanding beyond the call of duty; to family and
friends, who patted my hand and told me I was wonderful,
despite blatant evidence to the contrary;

   To Stan Middleton, for breaking his own rules and
opening a box of memories he had sealed shut and to his
wife, Renee, for encouraging him to do so; to Dorothy's
uncles and aunts, Ted and Mary Yardley and Jack and Nora
Smith, who submitted to endless questions with patience
and a modest amazement that what 'people like us' had to
say could possibly be of any interest; to Major General Sir

Digby Raeburn, for his time, his courtesy and for producing maps and battle plans; to Gene O'Neill and Matt Guymer, for soldierly insights;

To John Waugh, publicity manager at Armitage Shanks Limited, who provided the photographs of Edward Johns; to Alec Neal and members of the Landor Society for local information; to the Lieutenant-Colonel Commanding Scots Guards for permission to reproduce extracts from regimental histories and to the staff of the Scots Guards regimental records office, the staff of the Imperial War Museum reference library, the staff of Staffordshire county records office and the William Salt Library at Stafford and librarians at Stafford, Rugeley and Lichfield, who all produced documents, information and books with minimum fuss and maximum speed and efficiency;

To all those who were buttonholed, pestered and ear-bashed; to Mike Petty and Jenny Parrott at Bloomsbury, for enthusiasm, encouragement and patience;

My heartfelt and grateful thanks.